PENGUI...
SPIN AND O...

Born in Dehra Dun in 1958, Ramach... in those two great cricketing centres, Delhi and Bangalore. Here he once bowled in the nets to Mohinder Amarnath and twice shook hands with G. R. Viswanath. He has neither met nor bowled to Sunil Gavaskar, two of the reasons why he has such deeply ambivalent feelings about Bombay cricket. Of his previous book, *Wickets in the East*, a Bombay critic remarked that 'the rather lavish praise Guha heaps on cricketers from Karnataka may be the harbinger of another Cauvery dispute.'

A historian and writer on environmental affairs, Ramachandra Guha was most recently a Professorial Fellow at the Centre for Contemporary Studies of the Nehru Memorial Museum and Library. He writes on environmental history to make a living and on cricket to live.

Ramachandra Guha

Spin And Other Turns

Indian Cricket's Coming of Age

PENGUIN BOOKS

Penguin Books India (P) Ltd., 210, Chiranjiv Tower, 43, Nehru Place, New Delhi 110 019, Inc
Penguin Books Ltd., 27 Wrights Lane, London W8 5TZ, UK
Penguin Books USA Inc., 375 Hudson Street, New York, NY 10014, USA
Penguin Books Australia Ltd., Ringwood, Victoria, Australia
Penguin Books Canada Ltd., 10 Alcorn Avenue, Suite 300, Toronto, Ontario M4V 3B2, Cana
Penguin Books (NZ) Ltd., 182-190 Wairau Road, Auckland 10, New Zealand

First published by Penguin Books India (P) Ltd. 1994

Typeset in Palatino by Digital Technologies and Printing Solutions, New Delhi

For S.C. Bhargava
professor of physics and integrity at St. Stephen's College, Delhi

Cricket has responded, as ever, to the *Zeitgeist*; it has developed a routine standardized efficiency at the expense of the personal touch ... It is offering itself in one-day hit-or-miss scrambles in which winning or losing points or awards is the only appeal to the spectator; for, in such circumstances, style, spaciousness and variety of technique are not free to show themselves; in fact, are discouraged. A slow spin bowler as gifted as Rhodes would seldom get a chance to develop his craft in one-day instant cricket. Imagine any subtly-minded spin bowler dedicated to a species of cricket which limits the number of overs he may bowl in the opponents' innings.

In 'instant' cricket there is no scope for the great architect batsman, the Leonard Huttons, the C.B. Frys, the Bradmans, who truly symphonized batsmanship, so that we can sit back (untroubled by myopic competitive blind spots) and admire the development, the transitions, a comprehensive display of a master batsman's skill, with the fascination of style that is the man himself holding us throughout the day.

– Neville Cardus, in *Full Score* (1970)

Contents

Preface

Cricket writers are failed cricketers as much as art critics are failed artists and newspaper editors unfulfilled politicians whose last successful election was to the College Union. The difference is that we who write on cricket do so without envy. The success of an artist is quickly ascribed to the manipulation of fashion and the market; of the politician, to manipulation of the public or ballot box. But those who successfully manipulate bat and ball arouse only wonder. I have myself tried, and failed, to bowl a late outswinger from the edge of the crease; and tried, and failed, to hit a dipping leg-break on the rise over extra cover. Watching Kapil Dev carry off one or the other, I have gloried unashamedly in the achievement. To fail at art or politics is to embitter one for life; to fail on the cricket field is to marvel at those who don't.

This book is centred on the great Indian cricketers of the Seventies: men who played for state and country even as I was playing, with a good deal less success, for club and college. Like *Wickets in the East*, my previous study of cricket in India, it draws most of all on personal memories and on folklore handed down from generation to generation. I have benefited immeasurably from the kindness and wisdom of three Old Cricketers: N. Duraiswami, who once fielded brilliantly, one-handed, for St. Stephen's College; Sujit Mukherjee, who used to bat doggedly down the middle order for Bihar; and

V.M. Muddiah, who spun many an artful off-break for Services and for India. I have also to thank my friend and former teammate, Amrit Mathur, who read the manuscript with the critical eye of a high cricket administrator. My final debt is to a man I never knew: the late K.V. Gopalaratnam, from whose collection of clippings and souvenirs, now housed at the library of the Sports Authority of India, I have garnered some of the choicest stories in the book.

CHAPTER ONE

Coming of Age

In November 1988, I decided to flee New Delhi and the sesquicentennial of the *Times of India*. Arriving in Melbourne, I found that city's most famous institution, the Melbourne Cricket Club, celebrating one hundred and fifty years of its existence. The second floor of the clubhouse at the Melbourne Cricket Ground (MCG) housed a magnificent pictorial exhibition, through which I was escorted by a kindly old man, an admirer of 'your great prince Ranji, whom we called Run-get-sinhji.'

My guide could not claim to have seen K.S. Ranjitsinhji in the flesh, but as we looked out at the vast amphitheatre, our tour ended, he told me of how he had first come to the MCG, a boy of twelve from the bush, to watch Don Bradman bat. This was the second Test of the famous Bodyline series of 1932–3, the first match of which Bradman missed owing to a dispute with the Australian Cricket Board. Bowling fast leg-theory, D.R. Jardine's Englishmen had easily won the first Test. The Australians now looked to their batting hero (with whom in mind Bodyline had originally been designed) to redeem national honour in Melbourne. Thus the atmosphere at the ground was unusually charged when Bradman came out to bat early on the second day. Fully fifty-five years later, my host recalled for me the Don's slow, circular walk to the wicket, getting himself accustomed to the glare. The batsman, and the seventy thousand spectators present, expected a bouncer first ball. Even as Bill Bowes approached the crease, Bradman had moved his right foot towards the off-side, in preparation for the hook shot. But the England fast bowler, in a classic piece of double-bluff, pitched the ball well up; too late to change his stroke, the batsman could only drag the ball on to his wickets.

Coming when it did, Bradman's only first ball duck in Test cricket ranks as one of the more dramatic moments in Australian cricket history. To hear an eyewitness account of that dismissal at the venue where it occurred, and surrounded by historic pictures, was an experience to cherish. Or so I thought, till a Melbourne academic to whom I recounted the story told me: 'Don't you believe that man. I bet all Aussies over sixty claim they were at the MCG that day.'

This was a remark to ponder. For many thousand Englishmen must likewise have claimed to have seen Bradman's last Test innings—a second ball duck, at The Oval in 1948—and I dare say Jamaica's entire middle-aged population was present when Garfield Sobers scored 365 not out at Sabina Park, Kingston, against Pakistan in the winter of 1957–8. More recently, fifty thousand Indians have since asserted their presence at the 1983 World Cup final, played on a ground seating barely half that number.

Cricket literature is so rich in graphic description that these claims can be confidently made, if only one is the right age and could plausibly have been in the right place at the right time (television and live coverage have made it easier still). My Melbourne guide had doubtless read accounts of that dismissal penned by the two chief actors—Bradman and Bowes—as well as the description in the classic study of Bodyline by Jack Fingleton, who also played in the match. But *I was there* has a moral force lacking in 'I have heard (or read) that'; brought up on Bowes and Fingleton myself, I was captivated by what was presented as an authentic, eyewitness account of one of the Don's few failures.

II

As a personal celebration of the great Indian cricketers of the modern age, this book is based in good part on my own, 'eyewitness' experiences. You see, I was not at Lord's that balmy June day in 1983, but I came of age when Indian cricket did.

Graham Greene once remarked that childhood, with its intensity of experience and imagination, is the bank balance of the novelist. Perhaps adolescence fulfils a similar function for the cricket writer, a reservoir of remembrance which he can always return to and embellish in his later work. Before the age of ten, an awareness of cricketing sensibility and technique can hardly be said to exist; and beyond twenty-five, one is either too cynical or preoccupied elsewhere, looking for heroes outside the sphere of cricket.

When the Nineteen Seventies dawned I was twelve, an age when cricket appreciation truly begins. When the decade ended I had just fallen into the embrace of Marxism, out of which I was to emerge, painlessly, in due course. In those crowded years I watched B.S. Bedi, E.A.S. Prasanna and B.S. Chandrasekhar bowl thousands of overs; rejoiced in the grace of G.R. Viswanath and the artistry of Sunil Gavaskar; admired the technique behind and before the stumps of Farokh Engineer and Syed Kirmani; gloried, as only one who was himself a hopeless fielder can, in the dash of Brijesh Patel in the covers and the courage of Eknath Solkar at short leg; and observed, with bated breath, the extraordinary Kapil Dev take his first steps in international cricket.

Corrupted by the wicked little men who now rule us, I sometimes wish I had partaken of the heroism and self-sacrifice of the Indian independence movement. But in purely cricketing terms my arrival in the world could not have been better timed. In his substantial if quixotic history of the game in this country, Mihir Bose has pointed out that prior to the Seventies, the story of Indian cricket (at the international level, that is) was one of splendid individual performances amidst resounding collective defeats. Later in these pages I shall have occasion to take issue with Mihir Bose's more bizarre theories, but this proposition I heartily endorse. Especially when on tour, Indian Test teams of the past could never quite believe that they could play on equal terms with their opponents. Nor did their supporters at home, who were happy enough to take pride in the performances, against the run of play, of individual members of the Indian side. We lost four-nil in Australia in 1947–8, but Vijay Hazare had hit two immaculate hundreds in the Adelaide Test, against an attack led by Keith Miller and Ray Lindwall. Fiery Freddie Trueman had run amuck when we toured England in 1952, but at least Vijay Manjrekar and Hazare, again, had stood firm among the ruins, while Vinoo Mankad, with scores of 72 and 184 and five wickets in the Lord's Test, had inscribed his name in cricket history in letters of gold. Although his side lost comprehensively in England in 1959 and 1967, in the West Indies in 1962, and in Australia in 1967–8, the Indian cricket follower of the day could likewise fall back upon defiant batting displays by some of his countrymen and, more rarely, on fine bowling performances.

A consequence of this was that foreign cricketers acquired a larger-than-life image in the eyes of Indian players and fans. Thus on his return from the 1947 tour of Australia, the wicket-keeper P. Sen returned to his native Calcutta, where he was felicitated by his club, Kalighat. Welcoming the Indian stumper, the club chairman referred to the Test at Melbourne where in a huge Australian score of 575 for 8, Sen had conceded only four byes, in a display of great skill and unflagging concentration extending over a day and a half. Replying to these words of praise, the wicket-keeper remarked only that in all that while, but five balls had passed the bat.

The next year, Bradman's Australian side toured England, the great man's farewell to cricket that is so evocatively described in Jack Fingleton's book *Brightly Fades the Don.* Huge crowds flocked to see Bradman and his team wherever they played; in Oxford, entrance money was charged for the first time in the university's history. An Indian journalist visiting England, cricket mad, was desperately keen to see Bradman play. Through his contacts in Fleet Street he was able to get a ticket for one day of the Trent Bridge Test, but all hotel rooms were booked. Determined to watch the Australians, he spent the night in a room at the Nottingham Jail, at the invitation of the prison warden.

The journalist was Devdas Gandhi, then editor of the *Hindustan Times*, and it is wonderfully appropriate that a son of the Mahatma be given free accommodation in a British prison—to see Bradman bat. This adulation of the Australian champion was widely shared by Gandhi's countrymen. The Don was of course the greatest of all batsmen, his side of 1947–8 arguably the finest Test team in cricket history. Yet in Indian eyes an aura scarcely less luminous surrounded the figures of players such as Len Hutton and Denis Compton, of England; and Weekes, Worrell and Walcott, of the West Indies. Like Bradman, they had been elevated to a status at least equivalent to the major gods of the Hindu pantheon.

This reverence was not restricted to the fans alone. In 1967, three young Bangalore cricketers—V. Subrahmanyam, E.A.S. Prasanna and B.S. Chandrasekhar—were selected to tour England with the Indian team. They were immediately summoned by an older fellow townsman, who had played, in 1932, on India's first official tour of England. This veteran ordered the trio to put on a bagful of sweaters, whereupon they all marched off to the Central College ground. Here the groundsman had already been instructed to pour bucketfuls of water on the wicket. The climate and playing conditions in England so mimicked, the three cricketers were made to bat, bowl and field on the soggiest of pitches. At length the old cricketer decided they had had enough. But as a parting word of advice he told Subrahmanyam, the batsman, always to walk as soon as he edged the ball (for English wicket-keepers and slip fieldsmen never dropped catches), and Prasanna and Chandrasekhar, the bowlers, to always add the suffix 'sir' when appealing, as a mark of respect for English umpires.

III

I do not know what the Bangalore cricketers made of this orientation course, though one must suspect it made them even more apprehensive of playing in England. At any rate, their team was thrashed comprehensively in the three Test matches of the series.

But on the next Indian tour of England things were all too different. This tour took place in 1971, the year which in many respects marks a watershed in Indian cricket history. In the first months of that year the Indian team, led by Ajit Wadekar, visited the West Indies, where on a tour nine years earlier they had been thrashed five-nil. Against a team led by Garfield Sobers—who in our pantheon then occupied a place adjoining Bradman's—the Indians quite unexpectedly claimed the series one-nil, winning the Port of Spain Test easily and more than holding their own in the other four matches. Next, Wadekar's side toured England, where the home team was fresh from a comprehensive victory on tour against Australia. On two previous visits to England India had failed to win or draw a Test, and in forty years of trying were still without a victory in England. Astonishingly, the success in the West Indies was repeated, with India winning the only Test where a result was possible, at The Oval (where, ironically, the match-winner was B.S. Chandrasekhar, bowling with but one sleeveless sweater on a wicket with no water in it).

These victories in the West Indies and in England were not, of course, the first time an Indian team had won a Test match or Test series outside India. Three years previously, a side led by the Nawab of Pataudi had resoundingly beaten New Zealand (by three Tests to one) in a tour of that country. A batsman of skill and courage, a fielder of genius, and a captain of high independence, Pataudi has an honoured place in Indian cricket history. By making spin bowling our chief form of attack, and by hugely elevating fielding standards, Pataudi helped lay the foundations of our later successes. All the same, that victory over New Zealand cannot quite compare with the victories of Ajit Wadekar's side against infinitely stronger teams in 1971—the year that must mark Indian cricket's coming of age.

Subsequently, India has won Tests in Australia—Greg Chappell and Denis Lillee notwithstanding—and in the West Indies, again, over a side containing Vivian Richards, Clive Lloyd and Michael Holding. There have also, of course, been some more, and emphatic, defeats. But from 1971, the expectations of Indian cricketers and cricket followers have rapidly risen. The admiration for foreign cricketers remains unstinted, but they have not been deified as Bradman or Hutton once were. This is a mark not of the relative calibre of players from different generations, but rather, of shifts in perception as Indian cricket has come of age.

That the Nineteen Seventies were indeed a watershed (perhaps even the high point) in Indian cricket history is brought out clearly in the following table, which I have borrowed from the *Indian Express*. In an essay on W.G. Grace, John Arlott explained that he had not relied on statistics, for he 'was concerned with greatness, not with damn dots.' That is also the approach I have followed in this book. But numbers have their uses; very occasionally, they might even tell the truth:

INDIA IN TEST CRICKET, 1950 TO 1993

	Played	Won	Lost	Drawn
		1950s		
Home	25	6	8	11
Away	19	0	9	10
		1960s		
Home	36	6	8	22
Away	16	3	13	0
		1970s		
Home	34	11	7	16
Away	30	6	12	12
		1980s		
Home	42	8	9	25*
Away	39	3	12	24
		1990s		
Home	5	5	0	0
Away	16	1	7	11

* One match was tied

From the Nineteen Seventies, then, cricketers from other countries were seen, perhaps for the first time, in perspective. Simultaneously, Indian cricketers began to take their turn on the world stage, wider recognition of their skills being greatly aided by the fact that their team now lost Test matches less frequently than before. Meanwhile, Indian Test players appeared with conspicuous success on the English county circuit, and

8

three—Bishen Bedi, Farokh Engineer and Sunil Gavaskar—
were included in the Rest of the World side that toured Australia
in the early Seventies. A more permanent indication of this
new-found status might be found in the annals of cricket
literature. Previously the achievements of Indians, K.S.
Ranjitsinhji gloriously excepted, had been underplayed, and
occasionally ignored altogether by Western critics: the most
striking illustration of which was the omission, in the collection
edited by John Arlott on *The Great All-Rounders* (1968), of an
essay on Vinoo Mankad. Only a little less contentious perhaps
(from an Indian point of view) was the neglect, in a companion
volume on *The Great Batsmen*, of a profile of Vijay Merchant.
Arlott himself was a great admirer of Mankad and Merchant,
and he had cut his teeth as a cricket correspondent watching them
play in England in 1946. But when he planned his volumes, in
the mid-Sixties, Indian cricket was at its lowest ebb, having lost
all Test matches on its last tours of the West Indies, England and
Australia—this might explain Arlott's inclusion, in his volumes,
of some other cricketers not in the same league as the Indian duo,
but who played for more successful Test sides. Of late, however,
foreign writers have begun paying warm tribute to the great
Indians of our era; no such volumes would be planned today
which could exclude Kapil Dev (whose all-round gifts,
arguably, do not exceed Mankad's) and Sunil Gavaskar, who
will himself tell you that he is not convinced he was a better
batsman than his famous townsman, Merchant.

IV

History and cricket literature alike are notoriously unkind to
losers. But for an Indian writer, it is impossible to see the great
moderns in isolation from the traditions of the players of the past.
Thus the first great Indian slow bowler had toured England
exactly sixty years before Wadekar's side, where his

performance was scarcely less creditable than the performances of Bedi, Chandrasekhar, Venkatraghavan or Prasanna in our time. And Gavaskar might have been the acknowledged batting superstar of the side of the Seventies, but behind the studied care of his forward defensive push and the awesome power of his straight drive lay a long history, associated exclusively with the city where he was born and learnt his cricket.

The art of slow bowling and the Bombay School of Batsmanship are, as I show in this study, the two Great Traditions of Indian cricket. These traditions converged with splendid effect at The Oval in 1971, in a match won by spin bowlers and with victory arriving the day of Ganesh Chathurti, a major festival in the city from which six of the first seven batsmen in the Indian team came. Yet that famous side also had space within it for a representative each of two other distinctively Indian lineages, our Little Traditions so to speak: the wristy batting stylist (here represented by G.R. Viswanath) and the wicket-keeper who is at his best while standing up (in this case, Farokh Engineer). Perhaps Kapil Dev, chronologically the last of the cricketers honoured here, might be put in a class of his own; but even he has had his gifted, if somewhat unacknowledged, predecessors.

By placing my heroes in history, I wish also to pay tribute to cricketers of an earlier epoch, and to the men who told me about them. For cricket chauvinism runs across two axes, those of nation and generation. All Indians will insist that Bishen Bedi was a finer slow bowler than his great contemporary, England's Derek Underwood—a unanimity that lies behind some of the more partisan judgements in this book—but any two, if separated by twenty years in age, might never agree on whether the Sardar of Spin was indeed a more accomplished exponent of the craft of slow left-arm bowling than Vinoo Mankad (in the inevitable extension of this conundrum, my eight-year-old nephew recently asked me: 'Was Bedi really as good as Maninder Singh?')

One might think that the act of comparison would tend to favour players still playing. For one thing, the deeds of contemporary cricketers are all over the newspapers, their faces smile out at us from posters and magazines. It might also be argued that tactics and technology have changed, indeed progressed so swiftly that older cricketers would have been unable to adapt to the game as it is now played ('Would any captain allow Ranji to have played the leg-glance?' asks the modern sceptic). Set against this is the deference in Indian culture accorded to age ('if uncle says it *must* be so') and the conviction—more powerful even than print—carried by the eyewitness account ('I have seen Mankad bowl, and I tell you Bedi does not hold a candle to him').

This is a game incapable of final resolution, yet for that very reason, so beloved of the cricket lover. When to one's hero a friend or relative juxtaposes a hero of another country or time, the contrast illuminates both cricketers in quite unexpected ways. In cricket talk, at any rate, comparisons are glorious. Through them one can see more clearly than ever before, what is truly distinctive about the style of individual cricketers, and what is better viewed as a creative elaboration of a longstanding tradition. One might even be persuaded of two propositions that have taken me twenty years to accept: that there were Indian spin bowlers before Bishen Bedi, and that there will be Indian batsmen after Sunil Gavaskar.

CHAPTER TWO

The Holy Trinity

O n Bishen Bedi's last tour of England, as manager of the Indian cricket team of 1990, the sportswriter Frank Keating likened him to Friar Tuck. Like that legendary figure of English history, wrote Keating, Bedi was both round of body and genial in temperament. True, the Sardar of Spin has always been the most generous of men, but the whisky waistline he now commands is in fact of a comparatively later provenance.

When I first set eyes on Bedi, in December 1972, he was a slim figure moving gracefully in the field. England were playing India at the Firozshah Kotla ground in Delhi, and we had seats at midwicket, a vantage point normally considered inferior to watching from close to or over the sightscreen. But it was the ideal place from which to admire the beautiful arc described by Bedi's flight. Like English batsmen and Australian spectators, I was immediately struck by the ease of his approach to the wicket, the slowness of his bowling, and the heights to which he tossed the ball. The playwright J.M. Barrie, a cricketer of enthusiasm and indifferent skill, described his own bowling as 'so slow that if I do not like a ball I can run after it and bring it back.' Or so recounted Neville Cardus, who might very well have recalled the playwright when he saw Bishen Bedi bowl many years later. For Bedi flighted the ball higher than any bowler in international cricket: if he could challenge quick-footed batsmen thus, it was only because (unlike Barrie) his command was so complete that he would make the ball descend far quicker than it went up.

In later years, I often watched Bedi bowl from a position closer to the sightscreen. While the arc looked less exquisite from this angle, one could now more fully understand why most batsmen preferred to play him from the safety of the crease. Their timidity did not stop Bedi from beating the bat, even in Test cricket, almost once every over. The illusion of innocence created by the gentle curve was rapidly dispelled as the ball on pitching turned and darted past the outside edge. Bedi was apparently the slowest of slow bowlers, yet he made more haste off the wicket than spinners who looked to be twice as fast through the air. His nip came from a perfectly modulated run up, a classical, high and side on action, and a quick arm. This last element was perhaps the most crucial, for as I learnt from reading the critic E.M. Wellings, most great spinners have had a fast arm, which lends deception to their flight and makes for pace off the pitch. Bedi splendidly fulfilled Wellings' criteria, as he did the test laid down to me by my own first cricket coach—namely, that no spinner should be so slow that on beating the bat and wicket-keeper, the ball does not run away to the boundary for four byes.

It was infinitely easier to play Bedi with a pen from the Press Box than with a bat from twenty-two yards away. Reporting a Marylebone Cricket Club (MCC) tour of India in 1972–3, the sage Mike Brearley came down heavily on those English batsmen who played the left-arm spinner from the safety of the crease. Brearley himself was yet to play in a Test match, but with the confidence of a Cambridge philosophy don lectured his countrymen on how to use their feet to go down the wicket and dominate the Indian slow bowler. Next summer, Bedi joined Northamptonshire to play in the English County Championship. An early season match against Middlesex, Brearley's team, gave the future England captain the chance to put his bat and feet where his pen had directed them to be. In Bedi's first over to him Brearley jumped down the wicket but was beaten by flight and turn, to be comfortably stumped.

That great English off-spinner, Jim Laker, once remarked that his idea of Paradise was Lord's Cricket Ground, bathed in sunshine, with Ray Lindwall bowling at one end and Bishen Bedi at the other. (This is a nice image, coupling the fast and slow bowler most remembered for their classical actions; but it is an image I also cherish for its splendid indifference to batsmen, who Laker apparently thought had no place in Heaven at all.) Indeed, Bedi can only be described as a magical bowler. No slow bowler in living memory has commanded a more graceful action, more glorious flight, or—especially on good wickets—more prodigious spin. Above all, he revelled in his craft. I can picture, as I write, the Sardar of Spin at the top of his run up. He pushes up the steel bangle on his right arm and sets off, easily but purposefully, on his diagonal five step run. From the edge of the crease, he bowls a ball of perfect length on the leg stump, that spins sharply to take a tentative edge towards the slips. At the end of his follow through the Sardar pauses thoughtfully and then, still balancing on his toes, sways backwards from the waist: a characteristic gesture when he has the batsman in trouble, but not yet out. He then briskly turns around, thumps his left fist into his right palm, or (if he is especially keyed up) his left hand on his backside, and walks back to his starting point. Receiving the ball from the fielders, he pushes up his *kada*, and is off once again.

This is a scene I must have watched thousands of times, but I never tired of it. Bishen Bedi with the ball, and Sunil Gavaskar with the bat, were the two most *perfect* cricketers of modern times. One could not watch them play without wishing every moment was being filmed for posterity. Their methods were classical, with a grace and symmetry of movement denied to less orthodox but equally gifted practitioners of their craft, for example Derek Underwood and Vivian Richards.

Unlike Gavaskar though, Bedi did not take good care of his physique, and in the last years of his career his art declined almost as quickly as his waistline thickened. In his amiable, but cricket-filled retirement, he has a distinctly rotund appearance, prompting the comparison to Friar Tuck. But whereas the expansiveness of Bedi's physical form is a recent occurrence, that of his character is not. From his earliest days as a player, Bedi, like most Sikhs, has been known to be both opinionated and generous to a fault. The first time North Zone won the Duleep Trophy (under his captaincy) their victory over the redoubtable South Zone—whose batting line-up included G.R. Viswanath, the Nawab of Pataudi, Abbas Ali Baig and M.L. Jaisimha—owed itself to the left-arm spin combination of Bedi and Rajinder Goel. At nine o'clock that night, the shy, retiring Goel, his job accomplished, was fast asleep in his hotel bed, a *chaddar* (shawl) pulled in rustic style over his head. In his room Bedi was throwing a large party for both teams, tandoori chicken and whisky on the captain's account.

This story is related by the long-serving Haryana and North Zone off-spinner, Sarkar Talwar, and is intended as a tribute to both men. A less demonstrative example of Bedi's generosity came accidentally to my notice when India were playing a Test match under his captaincy at Bangalore in the mid-Seventies. The Indian hockey team were in the southern city at the same time, in preparation for a forthcoming World Cup. Where the cricketers stayed in a plush five-star hotel, and were paid ten thousand rupees as match fee apart from a handsome daily allowance, the hockey players were put up in a modest dormitory at the Kanteerava Stadium, and given thirty rupees per day for all expenses. Bedi, perhaps the only Indian cricketer who would have recognized the injustice of it all, took them out for dinner, I believe more than once. (Ten years later, a member of that

World Cup side, the great full-back Surjit Singh, died tragically in a road accident. This happened just prior to Bedi's richly deserved benefit match. Instinctively, but without fuss, the Sardar donated a share of his proceeds to the hockey player's family.)

Of course, the man in the street or in the stand was mostly unaware of this side of Bedi: he worshipped him solely for his skill at the ageless art of slow left-arm bowling. It so happened that the Delhi Test where I first saw him bowl, was also the match in which he claimed his hundredth Test wicket. Barely had the applause died down that our attention was directed to a splendid red banner that had come up in the thirty-rupee stand. It read, simply, 'SPIN HUNDRED MORE'.

I do not know whether in the excitement of play Bedi actually saw that banner, but he went on to add one hundred and sixty-six Text wickets to his collection. Curiously, when Bedi was asked, long after he had retired, which spell of bowling he most cherished, he chose not a Test match but an unofficial five day international, played at Sydney between Rest of the World and Australia in 1971–2. Here he bowled Keith Stackpole with an armer, and followed it by getting the great Greg Chappell first ball. As Bedi recalled it, 'The ball curled in with the breeze, pitched on middle and leg, and hit the off stump. I enjoyed that one.'

Prior to that delivery, Greg Chappell knew only of English and Australian finger-spinners, who needed a bucketful of rain before they could turn the ball on a first day Sydney wicket. It was, indeed, this prodigious power of spin that most marked out Bedi from other slow bowlers. An interviewer quite recently asked the Sardar how he came to turn the ball so much. 'Marbles,' answered Bedi in a mystifying one-word explanation. Asked to clarify, Bedi said that in his boyhood in Amritsar he had been feared throughout the town for his skill in marbles. Now anyone who has played that game, at least in the form popular in North India, will know that it requires, above all, a strong index finger to accurately propel your projectile at the enemy's. This Bedi quite evidently possessed for he had at one time a collection of ten thousand marbles, won from all the other little boys in Amritsar. That index finger next turned to cricket, to acquire 266 Test wickets, or roughly 400 marbles for each.

Bedi's benefit souvenir, which I once possessed, had assembled tributes to his skill from cricketers and cricket writers all over. Yet the most memorable compliment that I have seen paid Bedi appeared on a college classmate on Christmas Eve, 1974. This man, an archetypal New Delhi hipcat, wore patched up Levis jeans replete with phrases such as 'Make Love, Not War', and 'The Times They Are A' Changing'. Only one large patch on his backside was left intriguingly blank. Then came the Test series against a West Indies touring side led by Clive Lloyd, for the first match of which our hero was left out of the Indian team, on account of some trifling indiscretion on the previous summer's tour of England (as I recall it, Bedi had appeared on an instructional programme on BBC television without prior permission of the Board of Control for Cricket in India). On the morning of the first Test, played at Bangalore, my colleague came to class with the hitherto empty patch inscribed 'NO BEDI NO TEST'. It was a tribute the great slow bowler would have appreciated.

II

No one looked less like a cricketer than Erapalli Prasanna. Short and stout, with a perpetual scowl, he resembled nothing so much as an Indian businessman, selling anything from stocks to *supari*. Yet this was the man of whom Trevor Bailey and Fred Trueman, in their authoritative book *The Spinner's Web*, would write: 'Perhaps the greatest compliment that can be paid to

Prasanna is that he was even more feared by his countrymen as a bowler than Bedi.'

This tribute is even more remarkable than it appears, for off-spinners labour under far greater difficulties than other kinds of slow bowlers. By general consent, the ball leaving the bat is considered more dangerous than that coming in. The left-arm spinner has the added advantage of a natural armer, the wrist-spinner of greater bounce and the googly. Consequently, far more thought must go into off-spin bowling, and his physical handicaps notwithstanding, it was in this respect that Prasanna was most abundantly endowed.

Prasanna's action, while lacking the poetry and charm of Bedi's, was brisk and economical, and he too had a fast arm. I reckon he held the ball more in the palm of his hand than other slow bowlers, for his greatest skill lay (as Ian Chappell, among others, has pointed out) in making the ball pitch six inches short of where the batsman expected it to. This made for a goodly number of caught-and-bowled victims, and whatever his shortcomings elsewhere in the field, Prasanna rarely missed a catch off his own bowling. His powers of spin and bounce matched Bedi's, while his repertoire was neatly rounded off by a floater and a genuine straighter ball. Where the former drifted away late in flight towards the slips, the latter maintained direction but hastened through after pitching.

As artful finger-spinners both, Bedi and Prasanna were often coupled together in the popular imagination. Sunil Gavaskar, a man who played much of his cricket with or against them, has written of how at the fall of a wicket the two would go into a huddle, rejoicing at the defeat of one batsman even as they conspired against those still to come. Even so, Prasanna was far more withdrawn into himself than the large-hearted Bedi. I once watched a Ranji Trophy quarter-final in Bangalore where the two were opposing captains. Delhi required about 360 runs to win the match on the last day, and as Prasanna led the

Karnataka side onto the field, he passed Bedi, who called out in his cheery way: 'Three-sixty in even time! Should be a good match, "Pras".' The off-spinner merely grunted, and proceeded to bowl Delhi out.

Even when the two played together for India, these differences in temperament were readily apparent to the spectator. I can remember Bedi running excitedly to the bowler from mid-off, on catching a fierce drive hit off Prasanna by the West Indian all-rounder Bernard Julien in the Delhi Test of 1974, but can recall no such reciprocal gesture when the Sardar got someone out. Nor did the off-spinner ever emulate Bedi in applauding a fine stroke hit off his bowling. He disliked batsmen, especially those who got runs off him. (He was not a man to be often found in the opposition dressing room.) In that same Delhi Test against the West Indies, Keith Boyce repeatedly swept Prasanna off the stumps. The bowler played on the stroke, but taking no chances, insisted that the finest outfielder in the side, Brijesh Patel, be pulled out of his usual position in the covers and be sent to deep square leg (this was a tactic that would not have occurred to Bedi). He got his way, and in time Boyce departed, caught Patel bowled Prasanna.

Where my aesthetic side warmed more to Bedi, as a sometime off-spinner myself, the sight of Prasanna bowling quickened my heartbeat as nothing else on the cricket field. Only a journeyman knows *how* good the master craftsman is, and about ten years ago, I found myself sharing a hostel room in north Delhi with a friend who had spun off-breaks for his college—we spent the night talking about Erapalli Prasanna. Soon afterwards, I saw the man in the flesh, bowling in an India-Pakistan veterans' match. This was at least six years after Prasanna had retired. His figure now was even more unworthy of a cricketer's, but the magic remained. In three beautifully controlled overs of off-spin, Majid Khan barely got bat to ball. In frustration he at last moved down the wicket and (as I could have foretold) was beaten in the flight, but Syed Kirmani failed to gather cleanly and missed the stumping. At the end of the over Kirmani, who was still playing first-class cricket, went up to his former state captain and apologized, probably pleading lack of practice. The wicket-keeper had not seen a ball wobble like that in years, that is, since Prasanna himself had retired. And nor has anyone else.

III

One Sunday afternoon in the late Seventies, I was loitering around in my college corridor when a friend came up and asked me, 'What would you most like to see on World of Sport [the weekly television programme] today?' Without a moment's thought, I took two exaggerated, elongated strides, brought my hands together up in front of my face, ran five steps and with a final whirl, simulated B.S. Chandrasekhar's bowling action. 'Your wish has been granted,' said my friend. And so it was, a rerun on television of Chandrasekhar's demolition of the England batting at The Oval in 1971.

The air of expectancy generated by the arrival at the bowling crease of Chandrasekhar could not be matched by Bedi and Prasanna, who, although they took finger-spin to new heights, were essentially *orthodox* bowlers. Perhaps the most dramatic sight witnessed on an Indian cricket ground was of a visiting batsman beaten off the pitch by a bouncing Chandra leg-break, and Farokh Engineer (or Syed Kirmani) leaping a foot in the air to gather the ball. Chandrasekhar, 'the genius with the withered arm', made the ball bounce like a tennis ball, with the speed of Ivan Lendl's topspun forehand to boot. He posed problems for wicket-keepers like no other bowler, and it is a tribute to the skill of Engineer and Kirmani that they usually coped as well as they did.

Batting against Chandrasekhar, even for the experienced,

was a steely test of nerves. While facing Bedi or Prasanna batsmen could work to a plan, deciding where and when to attack once they felt sure of judging the flight and turn. The encounter between a quick-footed batsman and the great, but orthodox slow bowler might be likened to a chess game, with the overall strategy·being modified at each step as a consequence or in anticipation of the opponent's tactics. With Chandra the battle was joined afresh every ball. A googly might have to be fended off the hip, or rush through barely three inches off the ground. The leg-break might be bowled at the same speed as the googly, or come along perceptibly slower and with a late dip in its flight. In reserve, and exposed rarely but with devastating effect, was the faster one, going through straight but bowled at a pace considerably in excess of that commanded by the Indian new-ball bowlers of the time (this was the ball which, in two Delhi Tests four years apart, on each occasion knocked Keith Fletcher's off and middle stumps clean out of the ground). From the batsman's point of view, this was a game akin not to chess but to Russian roulette.

.His deeds on four continents are proof that when on song Chandrasekhar could run through any batting side on any wicket in the world, something that could be said perhaps of only two other bowlers in cricket history: the Englishman S.F. Barnes and the Australian Bill O'Reilly. But where Barnes and O'Reilly were both fiery of temperament, with a legendary hatred of batsmen, Chandrasekhar was gentleness personified. Sunil Gavaskar has written of how, at a key moment in a Bombay-Karnataka match, he was beaten on the forward stroke by a perfect Chandra leg-break, with the ball narrowly missing both off stump and outside edge. Where other bowlers would have exclaimed in agony (Gavaskar's was, as always, the prize wicket) Chandra carried on in his normal follow through, and asked the batsman as he came near him: '*Suna kya?*' [Did you hear that?] He was calling Gavaskar's attention to a composition sung by his favourite singer, Mukesh, wafting through the ground from a radio being played in the stands.

IV

It is surprising that no commentator, Indian or Western, ever sought to compare the great spin trio to the 'Holy Trinity' of Hinduism. Let us think of Bedi as Brahma the Creator, the deity who is everywhere but nowhere; of Prasanna as Vishnu the Preserver, the god who has numerous incarnations and variations in form; and of Chandrasekhar as Siva the Destroyer, who with the wink of an eye, or turn of the wrists, would destroy any or all of his opponents.

But think again, and the comparison could disappear as quickly as it came to mind. It is impossible to think of the colourful and effervescent Sardar in the abstract, as formless (Brahma is not represented in iconic form, and there is only one temple in all of India dedicated to him); there can be no greater contrast of character than between the tempestuous Siva of legend and the docile Chandra; and a bhakti poet would most certainly not be moved to break into song at the mere sight of Prasanna.

Crude though it is, I am unwilling to entirely abandon the analogy. For Bishen Bedi was in a very real sense the creator of the spin revolution of the Nineteen Seventies, the fulcrum around which everything else revolved. Once Eknath Solkar had bowled his mandatory opening over he would make way for Bedi, and the game would be immediately transformed—the nervously flailing bats of the opponents being met, when India played at home, at every unavailing heave by the 'ooohs' and 'aahs' of forty thousand voices. Bedi was on the spot from his first ball, pushing batsmen on the defensive before they could judge the pace of the pitch or think of the state of the game. To his captain, Bedi was completely dependable, for he never (or so it appeared) bowled a bad ball. A few overs later he would be joined by Prasanna, who maintained and indeed perpetuated this relentless pressure. Like Vishnu he came in many incarnations and had infinite variation. He used the crease even more skilfully than his confreres, and unlike Bedi and Chandra was equally adept at bowling from either side of the wicket. His glory was his control of flight: as John Woodcock once pointed out, in a peculiarly apt simile, he had the mastery in the air of a great kite-flyer.

Finally, when one or other of the finger-spinners was taken off, on came Chandrasekhar the Destroyer. Unlike Siva nothing caught fire at the mere blink of an eyelid, but the right wrist could wreak destruction with almost equal rapidity. In his report on that historic fourth day of the 1971 Oval Test, K.N. Prabhu imagined 'listeners back home glued to their radios as the [Indian] spinners set to work.' Alas, I was not one of them—then a lowly ninth grader in boarding school, and not allowed access to the common room and its magic radio after seven o'clock in the evening. The Indian first innings had just ended (at 280 in reply to the home side's 355) when we dressed for dinner, and on our return from the meal I turned reluctantly for the mandatory one and a half hours of study. My cricket mad House Captain, Vivek Bammi, went as per privilege to listen to the BBC, disregarding my pleas to let me accompany him. For a while I thumbed distractedly through my books till, minutes before we had to turn into bed, Bammi rushed into the study room to announce: 'England 101 all out, Chandra 6 for 38!'

That was an act of annihilation Siva might have wanted to claim his own. I also recall a more amusing occasion when again through no fault of mine I missed a radio description of Chandra's extraordinarily destructive powers. The Madras Test is usually played in the week of Pongal, the great harvest festival of the Tamil country. When England played a Test in Madras in January 1973, the visitors batted first and at lunch were 70 for 4.

After the interval Keith Fletcher and Tony Greig defended doggedly, and the Indian spinners were desperate for a wicket. Listening to the radio in faraway Dehra Dun, so was I. But then domestic listeners were joined by the General Overseas Service of All India Radio. The commentator, a proud Tamil patriot wishing to interest New Zealand sheep farmers in his ancient culture, began a lengthy peroration on the origins and symbolic significance of the Pongal festival, its colourful rituals and its culinary delights. As he talked we heard, at quick intervals, bursts of prolonged cheering from the Chepauk crowd. At last the broadcaster finished his disquisition, and remarked: 'Meanwhile as I was telling you about Pongal, Chandrasekhar has claimed three wickets, and England are now 112 for 7.'

V

Looking back on those years, a score of Test matches are imprinted in my memory: Tests won by the spinners singly, in pairs or all together. Somehow, the match I remember best of all was played between India and Australia at New Delhi, from 28th November to 3rd December 1969. After Australia had comfortably won the first match of the series, played at Bombay, India were saved in the second Test at Kanpur only by a battling 137 not out from G.R. Viswanath, made on his Test debut. The visitors arrived at the Firozshah Kotla chockful of confidence, and at a press conference before the match their captain, Bill Lawry, claimed they would finish the Test in four days, leaving a day free to go fishing in the River Jamuna.

Australia batted first and scored 296, the innings dominated by a fine century by Ian Chappell. Despite a dogged 97 from Ashok Mankad, India conceded a lead of 73, a substantial deficit on a wicket already much the worse for wear. The Australian openers, with that prospect of a free day in mind, began with a swagger: Lawry cover-driving Bedi and Stackpole cutting

Prasanna for boundaries. But immediately afterwards, Stackpole lost his off stump to a ball from Prasanna that went straight on, and thereafter the wickets tumbled. Although the captain himself carried his bat through the innings, in one afternoon a batting side of high quality was dismissed for a total of 107 (Lawry 49 not out), with Prasanna and Bedi each claiming five wickets. India were set 181 to win, but the match was not over for the Holy Trinity. Sent in as nightwatchman, Bedi played the most valuable innings of his career. He kept Wadekar, who finished with 91 not out, company for almost two hours as India won by seven wickets shortly after lunch on the fourth day. Lawry had his day off as predicted, but he was too distraught to take his rod to the river.

Perhaps I single out this Test, over all the others, because it was the nearest I got—one hundred and fifty miles away in the town of Dehra Dun—to a match won by Indian spin. (In fact, a quarter of a century was to pass before India again won a Test at the Kotla.) Through the Nineteen Seventies, as the Holy Trinity spun India to victories in Calcutta, Madras and other cities, I was always more than five hundred miles from the action.

But as it happens, my most cherished memories of the Holy Trinity have nothing to do with Test cricket. Coming of age in the Seventies, I was privileged to see three remarkable Ranji Trophy matches in which all three performed: three rich and close-fought encounters between Karnataka, for whom Prasanna and Chandrasekhar played, and Delhi, whom Bedi skippered.

The Holy Trinity notwithstanding, for me these matches were made memorable as much for the quality of the batsmanship. With the precipitous decline of spin bowling, the art of batting has also suffered a body blow. Thus where others of my generation might live to tell their grandchildren, 'You should have seen Bedi and Prasanna bowl,' I shall tell mine,

'You should have seen Bedi bowl to Brijesh Patel, and Prasanna bowl to Mohinder Amarnath.' Brijesh and Mohinder were only two of the most gifted players of spin bowling on display here: others included Surinder Amarnath and Madan Lal, for Delhi, and Sudhakar Rao and, of course, G.R. Viswanath for Karnataka.

Sometime or somewhere else I might wish to record or replay those three encounters in full. I might only note here that these matches collectively constituted the twelve most enthralling days of cricket I am ever likely to watch, not one of which I would sacrifice for all five days of a Test match, even a Test match against the West Indies won by India. Karnataka won on all three occasions (although never with ease)—results which pleased me, a lifelong Karnataka supporter, but which would perhaps not have surprised a devout Hindu, who knows that two gods are always better, and more powerful, than one.

VI

For an Indian who grew up in the Seventies, it is impossible to think that there could ever have been a slow left-armer more classical than Bishen Bedi, an off-break bowler as cunning as Erapalli Prasanna, or a wrist-spinner with destructive powers matching Bhagwat Chandrasekhar's. But how great were the Holy Trinity when judged 'objectively', that is, against the long sweep of cricket history? Here I believe that Prasanna ranks as one of the best half-dozen off-spinners in the history of Test cricket, alongside the Australian Hugh Trumble, the Englishman Jim Laker, the South African Hugh Tayfield, and the West Indians Sonny Ramadhin and Lance Gibbs (treating Ramadhin primarily as an off-spinner who bowled a surprise leg break). In an art more difficult to master, only the great Australian duo of Bill O'Reilly and Clarrie Grimmett were, among all googly bowlers since B.J.T. Bosanquet, as good as (or even marginally superior to) Chandrasekhar. Turning finally to Bedi, the Yorkshireman Wilfred Rhodes is a possible rival for the title of 'the greatest ever slow left-arm bowler'. I will not allow anyone else to be mentioned in the same breath.

I never watched Rhodes or O'Reilly or Laker, nor have I met anyone who did. There are, however, three contemporaries of the Holy Trinity with whom they might more readily be compared. One, Lance Gibbs, even held (briefly) the world record for the most number of Test wickets. With his high-stepping run, sharp turn, and bounding agility while fielding on the follow through, Gibbs was one of the most exciting of slow bowlers. I shall always hold him in the deepest respect, having watched him, at the age of forty, destroy an Indian side on a drying wicket in Delhi. The previous summer, I had listened in to the school radio (having by now graduated to the senior form) when his classic caught-and-bowled dismissal of the obdurate Geoffrey Boycott paved the way for a West Indies victory in the 1973 Lord's Test.

As one who relied principally on flight and turn, Lance Gibbs was every bit as orthodox as Erapalli Prasanna. But the bowler with whom Bishen Bedi is most frequently compared, England's Derek Underwood, was very dissimilar in method. He was truly unplayable on a wet wicket, prompting the joke that while other Englishmen had their umbrellas, the English cricketers needed only to carry Underwood with them in case it rained (this was in the days before wickets were covered overnight). But Underwood was much more than a wet wicket bowler. At his pace—a brisk slow-medium—his variations were perhaps not so apparent to the spectator, but the batsman was continually subject to changes in pace, flight and turn. I saw Brijesh Patel, that outstanding player of spin bowling, being deceived by a late dip in flight to hit a catch back to Underwood at a crucial stage of the 1976 Delhi Test, and no less a batsman than Sunil Gavaskar is on record as saying that, only with the exception of Andy Roberts, the English spinner was the most difficult of all the bowlers he faced in a twenty-year career. Rain or shine, Underwood fully earned the appellation 'Deadly', although on the last occasion I saw him, when the television camera caught him sitting in the stands in the Melbourne Cricket Ground during the final of the 1992 World Cup, his left hand carried nothing deadlier than a cigarette.

Where the careers of Bedi and Underwood almost exactly overlapped, Abdul Qadir's rise to greatness followed Chandrasekhar's departure from the international scene. As the premier googly bowler of his time, the mercurial Pakistani sent the same buzz of anticipation through the crowd. His action was equally dramatic—starting at an absurdly sideways angle with a lick of the fingers, then two elaborate strides, and a quick jump in delivery in culmination. Qadir was exceptionally accurate for a wrist-spinner, and bowled beautifully under pressure, especially in the one-day game. But he lacked Chandra's deceptive flight, and was harder on umpires and on his own captain than the Indian ever could be. Qadir also had the inestimable advantage of playing in an era when the best of Test batsmen—including, it must be said, some Indians—could not read wrist-spinners from the hand.

Gibbs, Underwood and Qadir all bowled in the wake, not to say shadow, of the fast men who dominated their own Test sides. Thus Gibbs provided accompaniment to pace bowlers of the calibre of Wesley Hall, Charlie Griffith and Garfield Sobers; Qadir to Imran Khan, Sarfraz Nawaz and Wasim Akram; and Underwood to John Snow, Bob Willis and Ian Botham. Only Gibbs, on the rare occasions when Sobers chose to bowl in either of his two slower styles, had a spinner of quality operating in tandem. Here their situation was far from exceptional, for the history of international cricket has been depressingly dominated by fast bowlers. Perhaps only Ramadhin and Alf Valentine, bowling for the West Indies in the Nineteen Fifties, and O'Reilly and Grimmett, doing duty for Australia two decades earlier, qualify as authentically great *pairs* of spin bowlers, winning Test matches and series all on their own.

It was their simultaneous emergence, as a trinity, that made the Indian spinners of the Seventies so distinctive. For the first, and almost certainly the last time in cricket history, Test matches were won with some regularity by a side almost completely bereft of seam bowling, and relying instead on a trio of spinners, all great in their own right and with skills that so beautifully complemented each other's. One might of course (like a good Hindu) have sectarian preferences, but in the collective consciousness of cricket they shall always be joined together. They were a Holy Trinity—Bedi, Prasanna, Chandrasekhar: Brahma, Vishnu, Maheshwara.

CHAPTER THREE

The Slow Men of India

While they presented a sharp contrast to the pace-dominated attacks of other countries, in the context of Indian cricket the Holy Trinity were torchbearers of a long, almost unbroken line of artful slow bowlers. Spin is truly the Great Tradition of Indian cricket, a tradition astonishing in its depth, persistence and richness of individual variation.

The Australian cricket writer Ray Robinson once joked that the googly should have been invented in India, for the very word rhymed with 'Hooghly', while the popular term for that delivery, 'bosie', might as well have commemorated Netaji Subhas Chandra Bose as it does B.J.T. Bosanquet. Writing in the Fifties, Robinson was perhaps the first to highlight the elective affinity between Indians and slow bowling, an affinity that has since been the subject of much speculation. The England fast bowler Bob Willis, a contemporary of the Holy Trinity, believes that the subcontinent's hot climate helps foster the patience and philosophical detachment so crucial to the slow bowler. For the scholar and cultural critic, T.G. Vaidyanathan, it is their proclivity towards the feminine that predisposes Indians in favour of spin, a quintessentially non-violent form of attack. And anthropologists of India, looking (as is their wont) for a caste-based explanation, have interpreted spin bowling as the expression on the cricket field of the craftiness of the Brahmin and the cunning of the Bania.

II

The first great Indian spinner—Mahatma Gandhi excepted—was in fact an Untouchable, Palwankar Baloo. Born in the town of Dharwad in 1875, as a boy Baloo moved up the Deccan to settle in Poona. His first job was with the ground staff at the Poona Gymkhana, where the English members sometimes allowed him to bowl at the nets. Baloo took as his model one Major Barton, a slow left-armer with a graceful, smooth action. Another member of the Poona Gymkhana was the well known Hampshire batsman, J.G. ('Jungly') Greig, who offered the ground boy eight annas for each time he got him out, an arrangement which must have maintained Baloo and his family for the eight months of the year when it was too hot or too wet to play cricket. Word of his prowess got around, and a strong movement arose for his inclusion in the Hindu team for the annual Quadrangular, played in Bombay and at the time the premier cricket tournament in India (the other participating teams were the Muslims, the Parsis, and the Europeans). But his selection was at first resisted by the conservative members of the P.J. Hindu Gymkhana of Bombay, the club which selected the community's cricket team. But class will out, and the Hindus did want to beat the Europeans and the Parsis, not to speak of the Muslims. After a protracted controversy Baloo was finally picked, with the Gymkhana members who chose him risking expulsion from their own, high caste councils. The slow bowler led the Hindu attack for years, leading them to some famous victories in the Quadrangular. In time he was joined by his younger brothers Vithal, Shivram and Ganpat, all of whom played with distinction for the Hindus.

Following his performances in the Quadrangular, Baloo

was chosen for the All India team that toured England in the summer of 1911. This side, captained by the Maharaja of Patiala, was in effect the first truly representative cricket team to leave Indian shores. In England, the All India side lost over half its matches, but for Baloo the tour was 'one long success'. In the opinion of a leading critic, E.H.D. Sewell, most English counties would have been glad to have Baloo in their eleven. Despite a persistent back strain, he took 114 wickets (at an average of 18.86 runs per wicket) on the tour and according to Sewell, 'With better management and better fielding would perhaps have taken 150 wickets and might even have headed the first-class averages.'

I recently came across the scorecards of that 1911 tour. Three early matches were played against Oxford University at The Parks, the MCC at Lord's, and Cambridge University at Fenner's. Lord's is of course the most famous of cricket grounds, while at the time of which I write Oxford and Cambridge were the great nurseries of English cricket, producing Test cricketers and Test captains by the bagful. On these three great grounds, redolent with cricket history, came an Untouchable from Poona, who knew only two words of English ('How's that!') and who in terms of social background was as far removed from the High Table as one could possibly be. But he could play cricket. In these two-day, two-inning matches Baloo got to bowl only once, for throughout the summer All India's opponents rarely needed to bat a second time. Against Oxford Baloo took 5 wickets for 87 runs, against the MCC he took 4 for 96 (his wickets including G.N. Foster and J. Daniells, both county captains, as well as the England Test cricketer, J.T. Hearne), while at Cambridge he had the exceptional figures of 8 for 103 in a University score of 434 all out.

Later in the tour All India played Staffordshire, where Baloo was pitted against Sydney (S. F.) Barnes, who is generally regarded as the greatest bowler in cricket history. The scores tell their own story: All India, 74 all out (Barnes' figures being 15/9/14/5) and 57 all out (Barnes, 12.3/6/15/9), lost to Staffordshire, 77 all out (Baloo's figures being 19.4/3/35/6) and 55 for 5 (Baloo, 13/1/23/2), by five wickets. This is a story, of Indian bowlers being let down by Indian batsmen, that we have come to know all too well. On behalf of the Holy Trinity, Bishen Bedi recalls begging his batsmen to get 200 to 225 runs—a total he reckoned would be enough for them to work with (the batsmen most infrequently obliged). Baloo's expectations were more modest still, for he apparently was satisfied with a hundred runs to his side's credit before he began to bowl. Even these he would not get that summer of 1911.

Baloo's presence on the tour was itself an extraordinary occurrence, for this was a time when the movement for the emancipatión of Untouchables had scarcely begun. That he was the first great Indian slow bowler is beyond dispute, but Palwankar Baloo also has claims to being the first Untouchable public figure. Proof of his status, in his own community and in Indian society as a whole, is provided by his membership of the three-member committee of the Depressed Classes, which negotiated the famous Poona Pact with Mahatma Gandhi in September 1932. The other members of that delegation were M.C. Rajah, a leader of the Depressed Classes in the Madras Presidency, and, of course, Dr B.R. Ambedkar. But where Rajah and Ambedkar had come to prominence on account of their social work for the community, Baloo could represent the Untouchables in the public arena solely on account of his record on the cricket field.

Palwankar Baloo must indeed have been an exceptional cricketer. The Parsi all-rounder, Dr M.E. Pavri, who often batted against him, said Baloo 'possessed both breaks, a curl in the air, and a lot of spin on the ball,' adding that he was 'the most deadly bowler on a sticky wicket.' As with Bishen Bedi, there was a beguiling innocence about his bowling, at least when viewed from the boundary—thus a Calcutta writer wrote of a Baloo over that it contained 'six deliveries—each a different menace—yet looking as harmless as the morning dew on a grass blade.' Another Bengali critic's description of his methods reads almost like a compendium of the cardinal virtues of slow bowling. Baloo, wrote H.C. Muckerjee in his book on the 1911 tour, was:

A fine left-hand bowler, who possesses marvellous stamina. Breaks from both sides. Has the easiest of deliveries. Seldom tires. Can bowl all day long. Keeps an excellent length. Never sends down a loose delivery. Understands the game thoroughly. Places the field to a nicety, catches come to [the fielders], they have not to go in for them. Decidedly a 'head' bowler.[*]

III

Baloo's last years as a player in the Bombay Quadrangular overlapped with the early career of R.J. Jamshedji, a Parsi from the other end of the social hierarchy who also bowled slow left-arm, and was the foremost spinner of his generation. A little man who turned the ball a mile, Jamshedji was once told by the prince of slow bowlers, Wilfred Rhodes, that 'if I had your powers of spin, no side would get a hundred' (Jamshedji could well have answered: 'If I had your powers of flight, Wilfred, no side would get fifty'). C. K. Nayudu, who played both against Rhodes and his great successor, Hedley Verity, regarded Jamshedji as the finest spin bowler he had batted against—high praise indeed. His fellow Parsi, the well-known commentator A. F. S. Talyarkhan, once described 'Jumsu' Jamshedji as a wizard who 'made the ball twist and turn in the air. It went round and round the seam as it came to you.' Jumsu knew all the tricks of the trade—before a match he would obtain some rosin from a

---

[*] See H. C. Muckerjee, *The Indian Cricketers' Tour of 1911* (published by the author, 1911) pp 20.

violinist friend, who used the substance on his bow. This the spinner carried in his trouser pocket, dipping his left hand into it every few overs to get a better grip on the ball.

In his *History of Indian Cricket* Mihir Bose has argued that if India has produced few good left-hand batsmen, the explanation lies in the subcontinental custom of using the left hand to clear the trenches after a bowel movement. This puzzled me, for if this taboo did indeed spill over to the cricket field it would also affect the supply of left-arm bowlers, who use the offending hand rather more directly. But Baloo and Jamshedji both emerged in violation of this history. So have the fine slow left-arm bowlers who have bowled for India since: Vinoo Mankad, Bapu Nadkarni, Salim Durrani, Ravi Shastri, Dilip Doshi, Maninder Singh and, above all, Bishen Singh Bedi.

When I pointed this out in a review I wrote of Mr Bose's book, a correspondent insisted that the great Indian tradition of slow left-arm bowling could in fact be an indirect confirmation of the causal connection between a culture's pottying techniques and its preferences on the playing field. The taboo, he remarked, could plausibly apply only to batting—i.e. one could not hold the bat the other way round. When it came to the act of bowling, Indian cricket coaches would instead wish to encourage wronghandedness—for a projectile hurled with the left hand carried with it the danger and devilry associated with all polluting activities. Let us not forget that the adjective 'sinister' (which must surely have come to mind as batsmen prepared to face Baloo or Jamshedji, Bedi or Mankad) is derived from the Greek for 'left-handed'.

IV

I leave that one for Mr Bose to work out. At any rate, no Indian is known to have carried the obligatory *lota* of water in his left hand, to pour water in the right. It is thus hardly surprising that in the generation after Baloo and Jamshedji, the leading Indian slow bowlers were all right-arm wrist-spinners. They included C. S. Nayudu and Amir Elahi, who also first made their mark in the Bombay inter-community. tournament (which while they played had, with the inclusion of The Rest, been named the Pentangular); and Sadashiv Shinde and Chandu Sarwate, both of whom toured England with the Nawab of Pataudi's Indian side of 1946. Among the googly bowlers who played for India in subsequent decades were Chandu Borde (better known for his batsmanship), V. V. Kumar (a hopeless batsman and field, but a marvellous bowler), and preeminently, Subhas Gupte. More recently, cricket lovers have followed the rapid rise and decline of L. Sivaramakrishnan and Narendra Hirwani, and the emergence of the bespectacled Anil Kumble, who despite an apparent inability to spin the ball promises to be around a while longer.

Compared to slow left-arm and wrist spin, the third great slow bowling variation—off-spin—took more time to root itself in Indian soil. India's first Test captain, C. K. Nayudu, while primarily a batsman of legendary six-hitting prowess, was a capable off-break bowler, usually operating (as W. G. Grace did before him and Sonny Ramadhin and the Australian Greg Matthews have done since) with his cap on. However, the first full-time practitioner of the art to be capped for India was the Hyderabad maestro, Ghulam Ahmed. A contemporary whom Ghulam usually kept out of the Test side was Jasu Patel, an off-spinner with a cleverly concealed but in the opinion of some, unfairly delivered leg-break. Jasu, who died not long ago in his native Ahmedabad, disappeared from the cricket field shortly after spinning India to a famous victory against Australia in December 1959 at Kanpur. At this time cricket captains of India could also call upon the very considerable bowling talents of Polly Umrigar and A.G. Kripal Singh, both batsmen-off-spinners in the tradition of C.K. Nayudu. Then in the Nineteen

Sixties Prasanna and Venkatraghavan came along, to carry off-break bowling to unprecedented heights. Perhaps the best of the off-spinners since have been Shivlal Yadav—a flight-minded bowler in the mould of Prasanna—and his Hyderabad colleague Arshad Ayub, like Venkat flatter through the air and devastating on a crumbling wicket.

This is an impressive roster of spin bowlers, unmatched in the history of any other cricket-playing nation. There is the odd Brahmin and the odd Bania here, but outstanding slow bowlers have in fact come from virtually all castes and communities. If an Untouchable and a Parsi were its founding figures, the tradition has since been carried on by representatives of farming/pastoral castes (the Nayudus, Shinde, Patel and Yadav); Muslims (Elahi, Ghulam, Durrani, Ayub); Sikhs (Bedi, Maninder); and even a Christian (Borde). Here lies conclusive proof that spin bowling is, in the strict anthropological sense of being present everywhere and among all social groups, truly the Great Tradition of Indian cricket.

V

It is tempting to regard the Holy Trinity as the glorious culmination of this long and uniquely Indian tradition. But in the opinion of knowledgeable critics—or at any rate, of some knowledgeable critics above fifty-five—the tradition had peaked a decade earlier. To my Trinity they counterpose one of their own: 'Mankad and the perilous arc of his bowling bent to the assessment of batsmen; Ghulam Ahmed, tall and billowy as he moved to the bowling crease, an artist of effortless action and endless capacity for work; and the bantam-cock efficiency of Gupte, bustling with vagaries of the ball spun out of the edge of the right hand.'

These words are taken from an essay published almost forty years ago in the journal *Sport and Pastime*—an essay, written by a Paṭna lad, that must rank as the first considered assessment of this Great Tradition of Indian cricket. Starting with the early pioneers, Baloo and Jamshedji, the writer (Sujit Mukherjee) ended with an effervescent tribute to his Holy Trinity of slow bowlers. There was Ghulam Ahmed the off spinner, 'flowing effortlessly to the wicket with that delightful little hop prior to delivery, the arm coming over classically straight with palm and fingers cutting across the face of the ball.' Then there was Vinoo Mankad, his left arm 'an inexhaustible storage battery' that had 'electrified batsmen to swift and unexpected demise all over the world.' Where Ghulam had a long, graceful and rhythmic run-up to the wicket, Mankad preferred a short three step approach, 'soundless and unstriving'. With this he bowled sharp turning leg-breaks, interspersed with an arm ball which drifted in 'as unannounced as the breeze which springs up at midnight,' or a faster ball which 'scuttled from the pitch like a worried rabbit.' Finally, there was the diminutive Subhas Gupte, only five feet four inches tall, 'with his brisk six-yard run to the wicket and the vicious wrist-action that provoked some turn out of the most unresponsive of wickets.'[*]

Even one who is too young to have watched them will recognize that Vinoo Mankad, slow left-arm, Ghulam Ahmed, right-arm off-spin, and Subhas Gupte, right-arm leg-break googly, must have all been truly great bowlers. Indeed, in purely statistical terms their record is not noticeably inferior to those who followed in their wake, whether reckoned in terms of runs per wicket or wickets per Test. Thus Mankad had 162 wickets in 44 Tests (at an average of 32.32 runs per wicket) to Bedi's 266 in 67 (average 28.71)— Vinoo also scored more than 2,000 runs, with five Test hundreds; Ghulam Ahmed took 68 wickets

---

[*] 'Skim' (Sujit Mukherjee), 'Toilers in the Sun', in two parts, *Sport and Pastime*, 12 and 26 February 1957.

in 22 Tests (average 30.17) to Prasanna's 189 in 49 (average 30.38); while Gupte collected 149 wickets in 36 Tests (average 29.55) to Chandrasekhar's 242 in 58 (average 29.74). And yet—speaking at least for my generation—in our imagination Mankad, Ghulam and Gupte do not quite constitute a Trinity in the manner in which Bedi, Prasanna and Chandrasekhar did.

Perhaps this is only because India won Test matches rather less frequently in their time. For one thing, Mankad, Ghulam and Gupte were more widely separated in age among themselves, and thus did not so often appear together for India. Vinoo (born on 12/4/1917) was fully twelve-and-a-half years older than Gupte (date of birth: 11/12/1929) and five years older than Ghulam (4/7/1922)). By contrast, Prasanna (date of birth: 22/5/1940) was but six years older than the youngest member of his Trinity, Bedi (25/9/1946), with Chandrasekhar, who was in-between, being a year and a bit older than the Sardar (born on 18/5/1945). These respective age differentials, as much as the rather less crowded Test schedule of their time, explain why the first Trinity played but eight Tests together for India, whereas the second Trinity played as many as twenty-four.

Then again, Mankad and company had nothing like the support in the field enjoyed by my Holy Trinity. The England all-rounder, Tony Greig, once observed that with Eknath Solkar at short leg, the Indian side had in effect four strike bowlers. As a fielder Solkar was out of this world, but the side of the Seventies could call upon, in addition, the skills of Wadekar at slip, Venkat at gully, and Abid Ali at leg slip—all marvellous catchers of the cricket ball. Contrast this with the Indian teams in which Mankad, Ghulam and Gupte played, when (or so I was told by an old Test cricketer) you 'were considered a good fielder if you caught a ball hit straight at you, waist-high; quite out of the question was the making of a catch by diving in front or leaping to the left or right.'

For all this, were two men, aged sixty-five and thirty-five

respectively, to sit down and choose an all time Indian eleven, most contentious of all would be the three places reserved for spin bowlers. Would it be Mankad or Bedi, Ghulam or Prasanna, Gupte or Chandrasekhar? When I put this question to the former Mysore, Services and India off-spinner, V. M. Muddiah, he refused to choose. But I was able to persuade him to discuss, one by one, the techniques of these three great pairs of spinners. To this most glorious of comparisons Muddiah brought an impressive range of skills and experience. He had played much of his cricket with or against the first Trinity, and in retirement had closely observed the second. What's more, as a retired officer of the Indian Air Force, he knew all about flight and turn.

When I caught Muddiah on the phone, after weeks of trying, he told me he would give me, at best, half an hour. But as we talked the half-hour stretched to one, then to two full hours—the most enthralling cricket conversation I have had.

We started with Mankad and Bedi, two left-arm slow bowlers with most dissimilar actions. Bedi had of course a classically high action, hand almost touching the ear, while Vinoo bowled slightly round arm, drifting the ball into the right-hander rather than looping it up. With his action Bedi bowled the armer with no apparent change in pace or trajectory, whereas Mankad's arm ball was faster and flatter through the air—easier for the class batsman to spot and keep out, but most devastating to the rest. Bedi had the greater deviation and sharper turn, said Muddiah, and Mankad slightly better control. The Sardar was a poor fielder to his own bowling, both because of his bulk and his habit of running diagonally to bowl, between the umpire and the stumps. Vinoo, who was a natural athlete, had a straight run up and thus a fuller and more balanced follow through. He darted about so quickly on delivering the ball, that at times he could even dispense with an orthodox mid-on and mid-off.

An earlier conversation had brought out Muddiah's deep

admiration for Ghulam Ahmed, whom he had then called 'the greatest bowler in the world', only incidentally because he had kept the air force officer out of the Indian team for ten years. But as a native of Bangalore, and a connoisseur of flight, Muddiah also had a lot of time for Erapalli Prasanna. In the air, he now remarked, Prasanna could outwit anybody, dragging the ball back in the flight almost twelve to eighteen inches short of where the batsman expected it to pitch. Ghulam, who was a taller man and bowled more side-on with a quick arm action, had nothing like the same loop. But he had perhaps more variation, a better concealed straighter ball and leg-cutter. Where the Karnataka man, owing to his marvellous control of flight, could get wickets on the best behaved pitches, Ghulam combined the roles of container and destroyer, and was devastating on a turning track.

We came finally to the two wrist-spinners. At his pace and with his unique action, Chandrasekhar bowled the odd loose ball, whereas Subhas Gupte was tremendously accurate for one of his tribe, having in effect the control of a finger spinner. Subhas really tweaked the ball, yet had great command over flight. When his great contemporary, Richie Benaud, bowled his top-spinner, it was a rather obvious telegraph signal, to be immediately distinguished by the batsman as being much quicker through the air; whereas Gupte bowled this ball with the same flight and pace as his stock leg-break. Chandra commanded less turn than Subhas, but had far greater nip off the wicket. He was also more tough—Gupte could not take a thrashing, and got easily frustrated when he didn't get any wickets. This was against the top order, but Subhas could dispose of tailenders with amazing swiftness, unlike Chandra, who often overwhelmed the class batsmen only to be held up by nine, ten and jack.

As Muddiah talked I could picture, in my mind's eye, Mankad come in with his round arm action, and pick up a caught-and-bowled low on his follow through; Ghulam, 'tall and billowy', bowl an off-break that went 'srrr' through the air, and on pitching turned many a mile to end up in short leg's hands off the inside edge; and the whimsical Subhas, with his angular approach and side-on action, send up a gorgeous googly that curved away late in the flight, but came back after pitching to bowl the batsman through the gate. Through a long afternoon Muddiah had played Sanjaya to my Dhritarashtra, helping me see our gods through his eyes.

VI

There is an uncomfortable caveat I have been dodging all this while, but I can dodge it no longer. Was 'my' trinity actually a quartet? The Sardar of Spin, its most vocal member, certainly thought so. When queried by an interviewer about his 'effortless action', Bedi answered: 'The basis of the fluent action was the movement of the hip, shoulder and pivot. But I would rather talk of the *four* Indian spinners of my time collectively. Technical correctness was our biggest asset; our side-on bowling action, the delivery stride and follow through were all rhythmical. We were proud of this and were collectively thrilled when any of us got wickets. Each was different from the other and there was no hint of arrogance among us.'

By contrast, I have in this study followed those two wise men, Trevor Bailey and Fred Trueman, who called Bedi, Prasanna and Chandrasekhar the 'Three Musketeers' of Indian spin, in terms of sheer quality to be distinguished from the man the Sardar, and some other commentators, consider to be the fourth member of what might instead be considered a quartet. I follow Bailey and Trueman in the belief that the man we have left out was a superior batsman and fielder, but not quite in the same league as a spinner. But let us now honour that great slow bowler and most selfless cricketer, S. Venkatraghavan.

Of all Indian cricketers Venkat perhaps best fulfilled the

classical ideal of *Mens Sana in Corpore Sano* (a healthy mind in a healthy body). He was tall and handsome, with a brilliant academic record—little wonder that the popular press in Madras had married him off to the dancer and actress Hema Malini (also a Tamil Iyengar) without the two having met. Or so I was told by my two closest friends in college, who were Tamils from the Madras localities of Kilpauk and Gopalpuram respectively. Both worshipped Venkat, their adoration made more complete when, on a winter holiday down South, one of them had been told by an uncle that Venkat held the season ticket next to his at the Music Academy's annual concerts. This was a man who had obtained a first-class-first engineering degree from the MIT (the Madras, not the Massachusetts Institute of Technology); this was a man who won Test matches for India; and this was a man who found time to keep time at a concert by Semmangudi Srinivasa Iyer. I understood their sentiments, but as a Tamil domiciled in Karnataka and, more importantly, as an off-spinner myself I could not bring myself to agree that Venkat should be chosen for the next Test match ahead of Erapalli Prasanna.

That disagreement aside, I remained a great admirer of Venkat's bowling. In fact, there was no reason—except the presence of Bedi and Chandrasekhar, and that there are only eleven places in a cricket team—why the two off-spinners could not have played more often together for India, as they did for so many years for the South Zone in the Duleep Trophy. Venkat's greater height made him a quite different bowler from Prasanna. He was much quicker through the air, with less apparent variation in flight. He was a less spectacular but, in some respects, a more subtle bowler. To the batsman, wrote the critic and commentator, Rajan Bala, Venkatraghavan was like a dentist, 'poking, pushing, hedging, provoking' as if getting him out was like 'the extraction of a stubborn tooth.' I best appreciated this particular quality one afternoon at the Karnail Singh Stadium in New Delhi, that most desolate and unattractive of cricket grounds. In a Ranji Trophy quarter-final, Tamil Nadu had conceded the first innings lead to the Railways and with time running out, needed to win outright. Venkat declared on the morning of the last day, setting the home side a bare 220 to win. With the support of the veteran leg-spinner Vaman Kumar, Venkat started prising out the batsmen one by one. On a wearing wicket he varied his angle of delivery by now going over the wicket, now round the wicket. (He was in fact a supremely effective bowler from round the wicket, a skill so sorely lacking in our present day off-spinners.) He got six wickets, and Tamil Nadu won with moments to spare.

Venkat's most frequent wicket-taking ball, at least on a good pitch, was his cleverly concealed straighter one. This either trapped the batsman leg-before-wicket or, if it landed on the seam, moved away off the pitch to take an edge to slip. I can recall my teammate Kirti Azad travelling to Madras to make his Ranji Trophy debut for Delhi against Tamil Nadu. Kirti is now a politician, currently serving in the Delhi Assembly as the Honourable Member from Gole Market, but even as a lad he talked big. Now he had visions of doing to Venkat what he liked to do to the college off-spinner (the present writer) in the nets. When Kirti came out to bat at Chepauk, Venkat was bowling. The maestro, who had done his homework, served up a short one, which was easily hit away to square leg for four. A similar ball came along the next over, but as the batsman made to pull, it fairly fizzed off the pitch, to make a mess of the off and middle stumps. When Kirti came back to St. Stephen's I consoled him with the thought that far greater batsmen had fallen to that particular ball—not least G.R. Viswanath, whom Venkat repeatedly had lbw or bowled in matches between Karnataka and Tamil Nadu.

In Indian cricket's coming of age Venkat had something more than a walk-on part. When India beat the West Indies for the first time, at Port of Spain in March 1971, he had figures of 5 for 95 in the second innings. While Chandrasekhar claimed 6 for 38 to win the Oval Test against England, four months later, it was actually Venkat who sent back the two best English players of spin, both classic off-spinner's dismissals. First Basil D'Oliveira tried to hit him over the top, but was deceived in the flight and fell to a fine running catch by the substitute K. Jayantilal at mid-on. Then Alan Knott got one that turned and lifted, and was brilliantly picked up by Solkar at short leg. In between, Venkat had himself caught a blinder at slip to get rid of the obdurate Brian Luckurst.

On his showing in 1971 Venkat was given a contract with Derbyshire in the English County Championship. It was an offer he could not refuse, but he was to pay dearly for it. Playing six and sometimes seven days in the week, Venkat drastically reworked his action, adopting less of a follow-through to conserve energy through the summer. Sadly, he was never quite the same bowler again.

VII

There is a goodly sized volume waiting to be written on the history of Indian spin. This book would of course have chapters on the pioneers, Baloo and Jamshedji; on the two trinities and on Venkat; on spinners with extraordinary Ranji Trophy records who never quite made it in Test cricket—such as C.S. Nayudu, Amir Elahi and C.S. Sarwate; on the great batsman-bowlers—Polly Umrigar, Chandu Borde, Salim Durrani and Bapu Nadkarni; on those the Holy Trinity (or Quartet) kept out—Padmakar Shivalkar, Rajinder Goel, C.G. Joshi and Uday Joshi—and on those who followed in their tracks—Dilip Doshi, Shivlal Yadav, Arshad Ayub, Ravi Shastri and Maninder Singh; and finally, a chapter on the One-Test wonders—Jasu Patel, Laxman Sivaramakrishnan and Narendra Hirwani.

This is a task worthy of a cricket historian with more skill and more diligence than this one. But having supplied a chapter outline, I might as well supply a title too. The book shall be called 'The Slow Men of India', with a foreword by the slowest of them all, Prime Minister P.V. Narasimha Rao.

CHAPTER FOUR

The Two Gavaskars

'I f Gavaskar had been born an Englishman,' said my uncle Durai, 'he would have been made an Earl by now.' This remark was not intended as a criticism of the treatment— not always generous—of Gavaskar by his own country-men, nor is it an indication of the continuing hold of British values on the Indian imagination. It was, rather, a comment on the pointed underplaying of the little man's achievements in the annals of Western cricket literature, itself so biased towards the achievements of British, Australian, and (latterly) West Indian cricketers.

I myself won a minor victory against this tendency when, on a wet April day in 1991, I first visited Lord's. I arrived just in time to join a guided tour of the Home of Cricket, conducted by a former Essex amateur with a vast knowledge of the game's history. Through the Museum and into the Long Room he was bombarded with questions from an eager Australian in the group, on the distinguished performances on the ground by his own countrymen. Our guide answered him with perfect courtesy, taking care however to slip in the odd remark about K.S. Ranjitsinhji's first century at Lord's, for Sussex against the MCC in 1893, and Mohammed Azharuddin's equally glittering hundred in a Test match ninety-seven years later. At last the Sydney man asked him the question that had plagued him all his youth: 'Who was the greatest batsman of the modern era, Viv Richards or Greg Chappell?' This was a problem to test even the most certain of judges, and our guide neatly deflected it thus: 'Let us ask our Indian friend what he thinks?' 'Actually,' I answered, 'Sunil Gavaskar was better than either.' 'No,' came back the Australian with a dismissive wave of the hand, 'he was too short to be a truly great batsman' (had he never heard of Sir Donald Bradman?). Our host more reasonably commented, 'I agree that he had a better technique and powers of concentration than either Richards or Chappell, but could Gavaskar *destroy* the opposition?'

II

There were, in truth, two Gavaskars. At the crease, the better known Gavaskar was a study in technique and concentration, cultured yet disciplined, unflappable in adversity. Bowl him six balls seaming away, and all would be left severely alone. Bowl him six half volleys on the off stump, and all would be driven crisply between cover and mid-off. This was the Gavaskar my Lord's guide wished to remember, and Western cricket writers liked to write about. This was also the Gavaskar his countrymen always expected to bat eight hours to save a Test match.

But there was, too, another Gavaskar. In this second, admittedly less frequent incarnation, the master batsman displayed a set of strokes dazzling in range and surprisingly powerful in their execution. Where the first Gavaskar refused to touch balls outside the off stump, the second Gavaskar could unleash a square cut worthy of Gordon Greenidge or his own brother-in-law, Gundappa Viswanath. Where the Gavaskar of legend always ducked the bouncer, this Gavaskar could play the hook shot to perfection. And where the more familiar Gavaskar never left the crease, this Gavaskar played spin bowling, yards down the wicket, as well as any batsman of his generation.

Although many of his great attacking innings were played outside India—among them, three hundreds in successive Tests in Australia in 1977–8, when Jeff Thomson was subject to the fiercest straight driving—the second Gavaskar has never been properly appreciated overseas: thus the comparison, a favourite one of foreign critics, between him and that obsessively defensive Yorkshireman, Geoffrey Boycott. This is a comparison his countrymen shall not countenance, and yet, not even the most patriotic of Indian writers have noticed the specific set of circumstances which enabled the strokeful Gavaskar to come into play. To be precise, when Sunil Gavaskar led India he preferred to bat in one style, but when he relinquished (or was relieved of) the captaincy, he could bat in the other.

The hook and the cut are the two strokes which, to use the argot of the literary critic, were 'indexical' of Gavaskar's style of the moment. Their absence was all too marked when he captained India, when he preferred to play almost exclusively in the 'V', that is, between extra cover and wide mid-on. When unburdened of the captaincy, the strokes square off the wicket came into play, to be put away as soon as he was reinstated to the leadership.

The contrast between the two Gavaskars was etched most sharply in the seventeen months between October 1978 and February 1980, a period of intense activity and high drama during which India played no less than twenty-six Text matches. India first visited Pakistan, for a three Test series which marked the resumption, after seventeen years, of cricket ties between the countries, who had gone twice to war in the interim. Led by Bishen Bedi, the visitors lost conclusively, owing to a number of factors: to wit, the waning skills of the Holy Trinity, the forceful batsmanship on the other side of Zaheer Abbas and Javed Miandad, the pace of Imran Khan and the swing of Sarfraz Nawaz, and—dare it be said—the partisanship of the Pakistani umpires.

Only two Indians emerged with much credit from this

encounter: Kapil Dev, whose debut series it was, and Sunil Gavaskar. In five completed innings he scored 447 runs, including two centuries, an eighty-nine, and a ninety-seven. Here he batted at times with an abandon rarely associated with the man. I recall one over from Mushtaq Mohammed—a wrist-spinner of high quality—in which Gavaskar twice pulled balls only fractionally short of a length high over mid wicket for four. I had never seen him play the shot before; the first Gavaskar would have played these balls, with a straight bat, calmly into the off side (the pull is in fact a shot not favoured by most Bombay batsmen). But Gavaskar was here in full command, and those two shots bespoke of both arrogance and boredom.

After the Pakistan tour the captain's head had to roll. After our cricketers had returned home, I was travelling by bus late one night when I read a stop press sign outside the office of the *Times of India*—'Gavaskar to lead India'. The visitors that winter were the West Indies, led by the gifted Alvin Kallicharan but otherwise depleted by the cheque book of Mr Kerry Packer. Here was something to look forward to: Gavaskar leading aggressively from the front, in preparation for the sterner test that lay ahead—the 1979 tour of England.

Against what was the weakest West Indian bowling attack in living memory, the new captain scored heavily and India won the six Test series, albeit by the surprisingly narrow margin of one-nil. Yet Gavaskar got his runs not with the flourish of the Pakistan tour but with a circumspection quite out of keeping both with his own batting skills and the calibre of the opposition. His attitude was perhaps deliberately infectious; in a long stand he had with Dilip Vengsarkar in the Calcutta Test the two men, obviously at the senior player's command, were much too cautious in their approach. When India finally declared, setting the West Indies 366 to win in less than even time, the captain had left it too late. To the disgust of millions, the match ended in the Eden Gardens gloom with the last West Indies pair at the wicket.

Anyway, Gavaskar's first series as leader had been successful and he had himself scored (at whatever pace) over seven hundred runs. Astonishingly, he was now replaced as captain for the England tour by Srinivas Venkatraghavan. Indian cricket history is ridden with puzzles, but this remains one of the most baffling. The explanation lies buried in the files of the Board of Control for Cricket in India, which will never be opened, and in the minds of its selectors at the time, who still won't tell. (The most informed bazaar gossip had it that the Board believed Gavaskar was contemplating an offer to join Packer's circus; they couldn't drop him on mere speculation, but—with the pettiness so typical of Indian bureaucrats—they could hand out a lesson.) Unburdened of the captaincy, Gavaskar did little of note in the first three Tests of that 1979 series, but in the final match at the Oval scored a double century which John Arlott (among others) has celebrated as one of the finest displays of sustained aggression in Test history. India were set a formidable target by the England captain, Mike Brearley—429 in a little more than a day—no side had scored that many runs in the fourth innings to win a Test match. In combination first with the doughty Chetan Chauhan and then with Dilip Vengsarkar, Gavaskar carried his side to within eight runs of victory (India, requiring 429 to win, ended at 421 for 8). When he was out in the closing overs of the match, playing a tired on drive in the air off Ian Botham, he had through an array of cuts, drives, hooks and lofted shots mocked the received wisdom (among English critics, at any rate) that he was but a technician of the very highest calibre, the 'Indian Boycott'.

Days later, on the flight home, the Indian cricketers were informed that Venkat had been replaced as captain by Gavaskar. In its timing and manner of telling, this was an act as crude and discourteous as the sacking of Gavaskar some six months previously. Two home series of six Tests apiece had been arranged for the winter of 1979–80: the first against what was virtually a second string Australian side led by Kim Hughes (for the Australian Cricket Board had not yet struck its compromise with Kerry Packer, to whom their leading cricketers were then contracted), to be followed by a 'revenge' rubber against the Pakistanis, who would by contrast be at full strength.

For almost the whole of that long winter, Gavaskar retreated into his careworn, captaincy style of batsmanship. Against the Australians he scored two controlled hundreds, and led his side to a comfortable victory. The series score against Pakistan was much the same—two-nil in India's favour—and the winning captain again led gingerly from the front, scoring two eighties and a masterly, defensive but match-winning hundred in the Madras Test (of which more anon). Then he mysteriously stepped down from the captaincy, and G.R. Viswanath stepped into the breach. The last Test of the season was a one-off affair scheduled against an England side returning from Australia, a match played in commemoration of the fiftieth anniversary of the founding of the Indian Cricket Board. In the third over of this Jubilee Test, played at Bombay's Wankhede Stadium in February 1980, Gavaskar deposited John Lever into the stands over long on. The left-arm swing bowler might still be wondering what possessed the normally sedate opener to act thus. The explanation was quite simple; someone else was captain of India.

III

A close study of the subsequent years of his career would confirm my thesis that the alternation between the two Gavaskars followed a clear pattern. Before he was first appointed captain for a full series (against Kallicharan's side of 1978–9) he was the perfect blend of rock-like defence and controlled aggression. No one who saw him bat in Tests played at The Oval in 1974, Bombay in early 1975, Port of Spain in

1976 or Melbourne in 1977 would accuse him of being the Indian Boycott. But then against Keith Fletcher's visiting English side in 1981–2 or in Pakistan two years later—both occasions on which he served as captain and leading batsman—he batted with exaggerated care but, from the point of view of runs scored, conspicuous success. After India had been thrashed three-nil by Pakistan in the latter series, Kapil Dev took over as captain. Now the second Gavaskar was again more frequently visible. Thus when his form and confidence ran low in the winter of 1983, he consulted his old coach at the Dadar Union Club in Bombay, V.S. Patil, who told him simply to go out there and hit the ball. Armed with this advice, he went to New Delhi to play against the West Indies. Here he hit a dazzling hundred (reaching 90 not out at lunch on the first day), repeatedly hooking Malcolm Marshall off his eyebrows while equalling Bradman's record of twenty-nine Test centuries. In the next Test, played on a brute of a wicket at Ahmedabad, Gavaskar hit a ferocious 90 in India's first innings, the first 50 of which came in only nine overs. This time it was Michael Holding who was singled out for attack. Ninety was also what he scored when leading India's victory charge on the last day of the Madras Tied Test in 1986—an innings that we remember as a memorable, late variation of Gavaskar Mark II. On all three occasions Kapil Dev—a man who has never let captaincy affect *his* style of batsmanship—was at the helm.

The enigma of the two Gavaskars is thus resolved, but why on earth did the little man have to take refuge behind his broad bat when he was captain? If we take the examples of three other batsmen-captains—Don Bradman, Ian Chappell, and Clive Lloyd—none of them allowed the burdens of leadership to inhibit their attacking instincts while at the crease, with highly satisfactory results. They all truly batted from the front. Gavaskar's very different approach might be attributed, in more or less equal parts, to the whims of the Indian Cricket Board and to his own philosophy of captaincy. While he played the Bombay man was indisputably India's finest cricketer and most acute cricketing brain, yet he was never allowed an extended, uninterrupted reign as captain. He was always conscious that were he to falter slightly, the cricket lobbies of the north and south would be at work, trying to replace him with their own favoured candidate. 'Save a match before you ever try to win one' became his watchword, and he knew that the most likely way of bringing that about—given India's notoriously fragile batting—was if he blocked from the front.

But it must be said that in this case the pressures of Board politics only consolidated Gavaskar's naturally cautious approach to leadership. Unlike his contemporaries Chappell and Lloyd, he was very much a safety-first captain, seeking always to slow down the game whether at the crease or in the field. So long as he led India he could bat only in one style, consistent with his larger goal of wearing down—or, in the hot Indian sun, exasperating—the opposition.

As captain and leading batsman, the pressures on Gavaskar must have so often been simply unbearable. Peter Roebuck, who was Gavaskar's opening partner when he played for Somerset in 1980 (in his only season of county cricket), once wished the Little Master best of luck before a Test match. Roebuck expressed his desire to see his friend score a hundred, adding quickly that he did not wish to add to his burdens. Gavaskar replied that since some 800 million Indians also expected the same from him, one additional person did not make any difference. A comment of grim humour, which I can well understand. For I have a vivid memory of watching a Test on television in front of a fire, on a cold January day in a village in the upper Alakhnanda valley. I was taking a breather from fieldwork, and India were playing Pakistan at Faisalabad. Having conceded a lead in the first innings of 280, we needed to bat a day-and-a-half to save the match. Gavaskar could not do it on his own, for he needed ten others to collectively stay that long with him. While he battled on his teammates came and swiftly went, one by one—only Mohinder Amarnath, a batsman as brave as he, stayed for more than a few minutes. When eight wickets were down the match seemed lost, but the seventeen-year-old Maninder Singh, in only his second Test, was determined to show up his superiors. He helped Gavaskar reach his century, defending doggedly for an hour-and-a-half before falling leg-before-wicket to a wicked low inswinger from Imran Khan. As the last man walked in—this was Dilip Doshi, as rabbit as rabbit can be—Gavaskar, his bat between his knees, sank helplessly to the ground. From eight hundred miles away I could palpably feel his despair, writ large on the small screen. The match was lost and the series with it, and—his heroic batsmanship notwithstanding—his captaincy too.

IV

My own longest exposure to Gavaskar Mark I came in a Test in Madras in January 1980. India were playing Pakistan, and I had tickets for the first two days of the match (on the morning of the third day, I was due to go by rail up the Coromandel coast to Calcutta, to commence my doctoral studies). Till that time, in ten years of watching Test cricket I had never seen India win, nor had I watched Sunil Gavaskar score a hundred. Two days were obviously insufficient to break the first hoodoo, but I might just possibly break the second.

Pakistan batted first, and on a typically hot and steamy Madras morning were soon in trouble. In a magnificent spell of seam bowling Kapil Dev dismissed both openers quickly, and then had the dangerous Zaheer Abbas caught behind for a duck. A lucky half century by Majid Khan and some pugnacious batting by the lower order saw the visiting side to a total of 272, perhaps two hundred less than they would have liked to make.

Gavaskar now saw a window slightly ajar, but he would open it in his own way and at his own pace. On the second morning Imran Khan, with his country's honour at stake, bowled at his fastest. To me, sitting safely in the stands, Imran presented a fearful sight as he raced in from the Walajah Road end, his hair flying wildly in the breeze. From twenty-two yards away he must have appeared more fearful still, but not apparently to Gavaskar. Judging the bounce and swing to perfection, he played about one ball in twelve. While he took on, or rather, blocked Imran, through the rest of the day Gavaskar saw a succession of partners play themselves in and get themselves out. Chetan Chauhan defended doggedly for a while, and Dilip Vengsarkar assisted in a half century partnership for the second wicket. G.R. Viswanath essayed a couple of wristy flicks, but was then caught at silly point off Iqbal Qasim, like Derek Underwood a left-arm spin bowler he was never comfortable against. Sandip Patil, on his Test debut greeted with an affectionate, elder brotherly tap on the shoulder from his Bombay and India captain, played two scorching on drives off Imran, but then hit a square cut hard and straight to point. Meanwhile the Indian captain carried serenely on, picking the gaps for ones and twos and hitting only the rank bad ball for four.

It was in the last half-hour before tea that we were offered a tantalizingly brief glimpse of the other Gavaskar. Imran's second spell was seen off much as his first had been, and with the front-line Pakistan bowlers visibly tiring, the master turned his attention to the part-time medium pacer, Mudassar Nazar. Suddenly the game came alive as Gavaskar, in the space of a few balls, hit Mudassar twice apiece through point and past mid wicket. He went into tea 75 not out, to the excited murmurings of the crowd of sixty thousand and my own rising expectations of seeing, at last, a Gavaskar hundred.

Sadly, after the interval his nerve failed, or rather, his resolve reasserted itself. In the company of Yashpal Sharma he played for the morning, restricting himself to the odd single down to fine leg or wide of mid-on. At close of play, after five-and-a-half hours of immaculate batsmanship, he had made an unbeaten 92, and India were well placed at 230 for 4.

Early next morning I gave the Chepauk cricket ground a last mournful look as I passed it *en route* to Madras Central station, and my train up the east coast. No one in my compartment had a transistor radio, and in any case in the swiftly moving Coromandel Express it would have been impossible to hear anything. I made desultory conversation with a Catholic priest sitting opposite me, back from training at the Vatican and proceeding to a parish in distant Assam. At last, at the town of Tenali deep into Andhra Pradesh, the train stopped for a crossing. Rushing through the corridor, I found a man listening to film songs on Vividh Bharati. I persuaded him to switch stations. Sunil Gavaskar, after almost ten hours at the crease, had just been out for 166, and the all-rounders Kapil Dev and Roger Binny were hitting vigorously as the total passed four hundred. India went on to win by ten wickets.

V

Nearly eight years later, I returned to Chepauk to watch India play Australia in the opening match of the 1987 World Cup. I had spent the past eighteen months in America, a country where it is impossible to buy a short wave radio or listen to the BBC. Thus I had learnt about India's fine two-nil series victory in England in 1986 and of the Madras Tied Test only when the Indian paper arrived, three weeks late, at the university library. I was hungry for cricket, and had slipped away without leave from my job in nearby Bangalore.

The visitors batted first. Geoff Marsh, that unattractive but effective opening batsman, carried his bat in an anchoring hundred, while Dean Jones and Alan Border blazed away at the other end. In the alloted fifty-five overs Australia had scored 271, a formidable total.

Gavaskar walked in to open the Indian innings with the local boy, Krishnamachari Srikkanth. As ever he wore a floppy white hat on his head, though specks of grey were now visible at the sides. In the late evening of his career—he had first played for India in 1971—one might legitimately have expected him to play without flourish; indeed, great opening batsmen, from Jack Hobbs to Len Hutton, have deliberately narrowed the range of their stroke-making (cutting out the more risky shots) as they have grown older. But Gavaskar had always taken good care of his body, his eyesight and reflexes had not declined, and most crucial of all, he was not captain.

The target Gavaskar chose for attack that afternoon was Craig McDermott; then, as now, one of the most hostile fast bowlers in the world. In his first over McDermott was hit on the rise through extra cover and twice, with that exquisite and inimitable turn of the wrists, past mid wicket for four. A couple of flashing square cuts and a straight drive down to where I was sitting, followed in the bowler's next over. This breathtaking cameo, lasting less than half an hour, ended when Gavaskar mistimed another drive and was caught at cover. With the Indian innings but eight overs old, he had scored 37 with eight boundaries. (The match itself ended in uncannily similar fashion to the Tied Test, with India losing by one run with one ball left.)

At the other end, Srikkanth, from whom the fireworks had been expected, was left speechless. This first match set the pattern for the rest of the tournament, through which the dashing Madras opener was consistently outscored by a man, fully ten years his senior, who in the inaugural World Cup of 1975 had taken all of sixty overs to score 36 not out against England. This late run of Gavaskar Mark II ended at Nagpur, when in the last match of the league phase, running a high fever, he hit a hundred off 85 balls against New Zealand.

Gavaskar had announced prior to this World Cup that he would retire after it (here he was following the advice of his early mentor Vijay Merchant, who had himself been careful to leave the field when he would be asked 'why' rather than 'why not'). India met England in the semi-final, a match played, fittingly, at Bombay. They batted second, chasing a target of two hundred and fifty-five. With his own score at six, Gavaskar was beaten and bowled by a beautiful off-cutter from Philip De Freites. Without so much as a backward look, and in his calm and characteristically unhurried manner, the greatest of post-war batsmen walked off the field for the last time as an India player.

VI

The greatest of post-war batsmen? To be sustained, this chauvinist claim requires that we exclude from our purview those batsmen (most obviously, Len Hutton and Denis Compton) who, although they achieved true greatness only after the Second World War, came to cricketing maturity before 1939. Even so, how does Gavaskar compare with the Australians Neil Harvey and Greg Chappell, the West Indians Everton Weekes and Garfield Sobers, the Englishman Peter May, and the South African Graham Pollock—six men who would all be on anybody's short list of the great modern batsmen?

Time and space are short, and I cannot go into a case-by-case examination. But it would not be impossible to demonstrate that Gavaskar's own record was superior, if only marginally so, to each of this great sextet: taking into account not merely statistical achievement but also the quality of the opposition; the range of situations encountered, and mastered; the support (or lack of it) from other batsmen in the side; and—a key test of greatness—cricketing consistency and longevity.

It is in comparing Gavaskar to his contemporary Vivian Richards that my confidence falters, despite the quickness with which I elevated my hero above him and Greg Chappell that afternoon at Lord's. My deeply ambivalent feelings about Richards were expressed, with reference to Donald Bradman, by a Yorkshireman some fifty years ago. This man had watched Bradman score four hundreds (including one double and one triple) in four Tests at the Leeds Cricket Ground. He hated Bradman, for so ruthlessly destroying England, but he also loved him, for showing him so much of his cricketing genius. When Bradman walked off the Headingley turf for the last time in 1948, having scored 173 not out as Australia scored 403 for 4 to win on the last day of the Test, he was met on the pavilion rails by this spectator. With tears in his eyes and admiration and loathing coexisting in his heart, the Yorkshireman exclaimed: 'You, you, you . . . . bugger!'

That is how I might have greeted Richards were he to have passed me as he walked off the field on his last appearance at the Firozshah Kotla. For in the three matches that I saw Richards play at New Delhi, each time he overwhelmed the home side almost on his own; on two occasions with the bat, and on one, oddly enough, with the ball. But I shall now take my heart into my hands and state that Sunil Gavaskar was indeed a greater batsman than Vivian Richards. For one, Richards had men of the calibre of Gordon Greenidge and Desmond Haynes to precede him in the order, and such as Clive Lloyd and Alvin Kallicharan to come after. Not only did Gavaskar have to open the innings, but he was forever aware that failure on his part could quickly spell defeat for the team: in this respect no great batsman (with the possible exception of George Headley in the West Indies team of the Nineteen Thirties) has carried a heavier burden. Richards had admittedly the more powerful shots, but his tendency to play across the line made him look more fallible. And where Gavaskar was master of all he played—seam, swing or spin—the Antiguan genius was at sea against high quality leg-break bowling. Both Abdul Qadir and B.S. Chandrasekhar—

and even, on one famous occasion in Madras, Narendra Hirwani—always reckoned they had a good chance of getting him out for a low score.

Most telling of all, Richards had never to play Caribbean bowling, at least not in a Test match. The West Indian pace quartet—of interchangeable parts—is now recognized as the most fearsome bowling combination in cricket history. A few, very few batsmen have enjoyed much success against them. Among those who have, the England duo of Graham Gooch and David Gower have each scored two brave hundreds off the West Indian bowling. More credit to them, and English cricket writers have written pages of prose in commemoration. Yet outside of India there is little appreciation of what must count as the most stunning of all Sunil Gavaskar's achievements: his *thirteen* hundreds against the West Indies, seven hit in the Caribbean.

Now, if Gavaskar had been born an Englishman . . . .

CHAPTER FIVE

For Country and for City

There are some batsmen who, in the popular imagination, are associated above all with one stroke: Ranji with the leg glance, Walter Hammond with the cover drive, our own Gundappa Viswanath with the square cut. This does not of course mean that these cricketers could not play all round the wicket, but merely that they played *their* shot in an inimitable and most effective way. I would hate to remember Sunil Gavaskar by one stroke, but were I forced to do so, it must be the straight drive. From John Snow to Malcolm Marshall, fast bowlers had only to overpitch slightly for Gavaskar to hit them, beautifully balanced and with a full flow of the bat, back past the stumps for four. It was a shot he played so often and with such unusual power that Indian commentators even had to coin a term for it. The 'bowler's-back drive', they called it, for it was at—or more often, past—the bowler almost as soon as the ball had left his hand.

Gavaskar has, only partly in jest, attributed the quality of his straight driving to the peculiar layout of the housing colony where he grew up. In central Bombay the apartment blocks are huddled close together, with only a narrow alleyway separating one from the other. It is in this corridor that boys play their first cricket matches, with a sawn-off bat and a tennis ball. Anything

62

hit across the line rebounds off a wall or, worse, goes crashing through a window, inviting the wrath of the housewife. A pull shot could thus severely strain neighbourly relations, and Gavaskar has even hinted that his mother expressly forbade him from hitting in the air. The straight drive was the most prudent of shots in the circumstances; to invoke the title of one of the little master's own books, it brought runs but not ruin.

Where his mother's hand can be discerned in his shotmaking, another formative influence on the young Gavaskar was her brother Madhav Mantri, the former Bombay and India wicket-keeper-batsman. There is an obvious comparison here with the famous uncle and nephew of Nawanagar, except that Gavaskar has always been too independent for anyone to have had the kind of impact that Ranji had on his nephew Duleep. Even so, his uncle's example was before Sunil, most memorably when the boy wished to wear an India cap and blazer that he found in the older man's cupboard. 'These things have to be earned,' Mantri rebuked him sternly.

Nowhere—not even in Melbourne—is cricket taken so seriously as in Bombay, and behind the apparent sharpness of Mantri's rebuke lay his own hard climb through the Kanga League (arguably the most competitive club competition in the world), college and university cricket, the Ranji Trophy, and finally on to the pinnacle of Test cricket. The nephew was in time to climb, with rather more ease, up the steps of that same ladder, but it was a lesson he never forgot. Through Mantri he also had a privileged window into the great Bombay cricketing tradition, the tradition from which he came and to which he has since been loyal. Gavaskar once returned from an overseas tour with the Indian team in the early hours of the morning; at ten a.m., he was batting for Dadar Union in a Kanga League match.

II

The greatest Bombay cricketer before Gavaskar was that other remarkable opening batsman, V.M. Merchant. Not long ago, I had the pleasure of meeting Brian Boobyer, an Oxford Cricket Blue of the Nineteen Fifties, since a pillar of the Moral Rearmament Movement. Having read something I had just written on Indian cricket, he remarked that he hadn't realized till then that Sunil Gavaskar and Vijay Merchant both belonged to what he called 'cricket's capital city'. 'Gavaskar and Merchant for an All-Time Bombay Eleven,' said Brian Boobyer thoughtfully, 'you wouldn't get a finer opening pair than that.'

Had he seen Merchant bat, I asked. His eyes grew misty as he recalled going, as a boy of sixteen, to watch the Indian touring side of 1946 play at Leicester. It was a typical English early summer's day, wet and windy, and the Indian batting was all out of sorts. But Merchant batted serenely through the innings, with scarcely a mistake, playing (in Boobyer's words) a series of 'the most exquisite late cuts.'

I was charmed. If that first impression could be recalled with such feeling forty-five years later, Vijay Merchant must indeed have been a great batsman. 'Was he as good as Gavaskar,' I asked. Brian Boobyer would not answer but with two hands around an imaginary bat handle, knelt low and, playing the shot as he spoke, murmured, 'Ah, that late cut.'

III

The 1946 tour of England was perhaps the high point of Vijay Merchant's career. In one of the wettest summers on record he scored in excess of two thousand runs, at an average of over seventy; always protected against the chill (as shown in photographs of the time) by a handful of sweaters, a woollen muffler, and a blue India cap pulled low over his ears. Merchant was not a healthy man, but he had to play in almost all the matches on the tour, both to keep up the team's flagging morale and to reassure his family in Bombay who (as he told his friend John Arlott) would think that he was ill if the British newspapers did not carry his name in their match reports.

In his autobiography *Basingstoke Boy*, published in the year of his death, Arlott remembered Merchant from a distance of almost half a century as being 'soft-footed as a cat, firmly built but giving the impression of gentleness rather than power, moving easily and powerfully about the crease.' He wrote, much as others have since of Gavaskar: 'Bowl [Merchant] six bad balls, and he would hit every one for four. Bowl him six good balls, and he would stop all six.'

As an apprentice journalist and broadcaster, John Arlott followed the 1946 Indian team—the first touring side after the War—around England. He thus had ample opportunity to watch Merchant at the crease: a masterful hundred in the Oval Test, innings of 57 and 111 (both not out) 'without detectable error' in that match against Leicestershire, and much else besides. Merchant's batsmanship was a key ingredient in the cricketing education of this most celebrated of commentators, but as it happens, the Bombay batsman had an influence on the Englishman's political education as well. In his own quiet way an intensely patriotic man, Merchant was a firm supporter of the movement for Indian independence. While the Indian tourists were in England in the summer of 1946, a three-man Cabinet Mission, led by Sir Stafford Cripps, was in India negotiating the terms of the transfer of power (prompting the Indian cricket captain, the senior Nawab of Pataudi, to famously quip: 'Mr Nehru and the Congress have only to contend against three Englishmen—we have to deal with eleven'). In an interview he gave Mike Brearley in the last years of his life, Arlott recalled asking Merchant whether political independence, in view of the inevitable partition of India and rising communal tension, was really worth it. 'Correct me if I am wrong, John,' replied the Indian cricketer, 'but was there not a man called Cromwell who had to start a civil war to enable the English people obtain their own political liberties?'

IV

From all accounts, Vijay Merchant and Sunil Gavaskar had uncanny similarities in both character and cricketing style. Mushtaq Ali, Merchant's irrepressible opening partner, recalled him as a 'very methodical man'—a teetotaller, non-smoker and vegetarian who, whenever he went out of Bombay would 'stick a small chit inside his suitcase detailing the number of socks, ties, shirts and other things with him.' This brings Gavaskar to mind, as does indeed the primary aim towards which this discipline and meticulousness were geared: better batsmanship. On the night of the final Test of the 1946 England tour, Merchant and his fellow Bombay batsman, Rusi Modi, were chatting in the latter's hotel room when the older man suddenly got up and said, 'I want an early bed as I have still to score a hundred in a Test match on this tour.' Modi suggested that this might not be so easy, for he would have to face Alec Bedser on a rain-affected wicket. Merchant merely smiled, said 'So what?'and departed for bed. Two days later it was Modi's privilege to be at the non-striker's end when Merchant brought up his hundred. It had been an immaculate innings, in John Arlott's words, 'characteristic to the last stroke.'[*]

At home, a great admirer of Merchant's batting was D. B. Deodhar, a critic with far more exacting standards than Arlott. On New Year's Eve, 1943, Deodhar and Merchant were rival captains as Bombay began a Ranji Trophy match against Maharashtra. When Bombay batted first, Merchant took on

---

[*] The recollections of Mushtaq and Modi, as well as some other stories retold in this chapter, have been culled from the valuable volume edited by Marcus Couto, *Vijay Merchant: In Memorium* (The Association of Cricket Statisticians and Scorers of India, 1988).

Dattu Phadkar, a promising young fast bowler later to have a distinguished Test career. Merchant came down late on sharp rising balls and chopped them down to third man for four. Eighteen and eager, Phadkar was sure that if he fed Merchant outside the off stump he would edge a catch behind the wicket or to the slips. A succession of short lifting outswingers were all cut away from the middle of the bat. At length Deodhar walked up to Phadkar and told him that he could never hope to get Merchant out in that fashion.

Nor perhaps, in any other manner. On that particular occasion, Vijay Merchant scored a mammoth 359 not out, taking his side from a precarious 90 for 5 to a total of 735 all out. Phadkar, who qualified by birth for Maharashtra, made a quick New Year resolution to transfer to Bombay (where he was ordinarily resident) before the start of the next season. Alas, this was not a choice before Deodhar. Even so, he must have greatly preferred to have Merchant on his own side, as he did when they played together for the Hindus in the annual Quadrangular.

D.B. Deodhar, of course, was both a cricketer and a professor of Sanskrit. Some years after Merchant died, the professor remarked that his friend's life mocked a famous theory of Kalidasa's. The poet had remarked that Lakshmi, the Goddess of Wealth, and Saraswati, the Goddess of Learning, were like two wives of a Hindu husband, always jealous of each other. (Kalidasa was writing aeons before the Hindu Marriage Act of 1956, which outlawed bigamy.) In consequence, both goddesses rarely bestowed their favours on the same person. But, wrote Deodhar, in the person of Vijay Merchant Lakshmi and Saraswati lived as loving sisters. Such has also been the case for Gavaskar. The one difference is that Merchant was born to wealth and Gavaskar acquired it (both men were born wise).

Like Gavaskar, Vijay Merchant gave no quarter on the field but easily unwound off it. As captains, both took few risks: they desperately hated losing a match. In an unofficial Test played against the Commonwealth side of 1949–50, India needed to time their declaration in the second innings to give them the best chance of winning the match. At an interval, Merchant told the two batsmen at the crease, Vinoo Mankad and Hemu Adhikari, to score quickly on resumption of play, then added, 'but make sure you don't get out.' Mankad, a cricketer of the soil, turned to Adhikari and remarked, 'That is like asking a man to sleep everyday with his wife but not make her pregnant.'

In another unofficial Test, played at the Brabourne Stadium against the Australian Services team of 1945, India followed on but batted bravely, led by Merchant and Lala Amarnath, in the second innings. When they were finally out, half an hour of play remained on the final day and the Australians needed a hundred to win. A tall order, but Merchant was taking no chances. For one thing, his opposition included Keith Miller and Lindsay Hasset, two magnificent attacking batsmen. For another,the match was being played on his home ground. Thus Merchant asked his bowlers to bowl wide of the off stump with nine fielders on that side of the wicket. Australia ended at 31 for 1, the match drawn. As the Indian side walked back into the Cricket Club of India, that normally reticent man, K.S. Duleepsinhji, called out from a distance of five yards: 'You have brought shame, Merchant, upon Indian cricket.'

This story is related to us by R.S. Whittington, a member of that Australian Services side. But Merchant, adds Whittington, 'was a different person off a cricket field. Later he was to be the main organizer of the publication of a book entitled *Duleep—the Man and His Game*, proceeds from which went to help Duleep's widowed Princess, Jay Raj, in less affluent days.' For all his doggedness in the field, Sunil Gavaskar will also be remembered by his fellow cricketers for his generosity, the readiness to help old players down on their luck by arranging a benefit match or the allotment of a subsidized government flat.

Befittingly, it was Vijay Merchant who as chairman of

selectors pitchforked a talented university batsman into the Indian team. In later years he glowed with pride as his protégé took the Bombay tradition of batsmanship to its greatest heights. Towards the end of his life, when Merchant was asked to compare himself to Gavaskar, he said unhesitatingly that Sunil was 'a far better batsman than I was.' Pressed for details, he observed that the younger man had faced better bowlers and of different kinds than he had and, moreover, possessed a better technique. 'During my entire cricket career,' observed Merchant, 'I was never able to make out the inswing from the outswing and the googly from the leg-break' (from the bowler's hand or action, that is) whereas Gavaskar made these discriminations with ease. Finally, Merchant presented himself as a safety-first batsman, who never took any risks, while Gavaskar had 'the rare ability of making strokes from the very first over. His advantage is that he is prepared to take calculated risks in his batting and thus able to score more often and faster than I did.'[*]

Those who watched Merchant in his salad days might dispute this judgement. So might two other Bombay cricketers who watched him bat only after he had retired from international cricket. Although the Delhi Test of December 1951 turned out to be his last first-class match, Merchant continued for a few years to play club cricket in Bombay. The wicket-keeper Naren Tamhane played against Merchant only once, but the memory never left him. Tamhane turned out for the same club, Shivaji Park Gymkhana, as did the outstanding googly bowler, Subhas Gupte. When their club played Merchant's, Subhas beat the maestro early in his innings, but that was the only mistake the batsman made. He scored a masterful 289, with strokes all round the wicket. Merchant's command over Gupte, the one time they met on the cricket field, recalls for me a remark of the Staffordshire and England bowling genius, S.F. Barnes. A

---

[*] As quoted in Dom Moraes, *Sunil Gavaskar: An Illustrated Biography* (Macmillian India, 1987), pp 181-4.

master of swing, seam, cut and spin, Barnes was once asked why he did not bowl a googly. He answered, characteristically, 'I didn't need to.' Were Merchant a less modest man, and were he to have been asked, 'Why couldn't you pick the googly from the hand,' he could have answered, with reason, 'I never needed to.'

As for Merchant's other claim, that he never scored off the first ball or the first over, we can counterpose the testimony of Sunil Gavaskar, from the only time he and Vijay appeared together on the cricket field. In 1964, the Bombay actor and director Zul Vellani shot a film, 'The Spirit and Technique of Cricket'. Current Test cricketers were asked to demonstrate different facets of the game, but Vijay Merchant was prevailed upon to show the late cut. (Vellani had been a student in England in 1946, when the batting of Merchant had warmed for him what would otherwise have been an unremittingly cold and lonely summer.) Gavaskar was one of the schoolboys asked to field while the masters performed. This is how he later recalled Merchant's arrival at the crease:

> He came wearing cream flannels which were then in vogue, immaculately dressed, boots polished and an India cap firmly pulled down over his forehead. He looked as if he had never been away from the cricket-field, [but] actually he was holding a bat, in his own words, after ten years.
> Kailash Gattani was to bowl to Vijaybhai, a few practice deliveries after which the [stroke would be shot]. Now Kailash in those days was not only sharp, he was also rated by the knowledgeable as the best user of the new ball in the country. He came and bowled a ball, short of length outside the off stump. Vijaybhai took one step back and across and late cut the ball to the third man fence. Pataudi, Wadekar and Engineer exchanged amazed glances while we schoolboys were left with our jaws gaping . . . .

Yes, that late cut.

V

The record of 'Vijaybhai' was one powerful reason why even 774 runs in his debut series stopped Sunil Gavaskar from getting a swollen head. But there were other reasons too. For Merchant and Gavaskar were only two exemplars of what is the *other* Great Tradition of Indian cricket. But where spin bowling has truly been a pan-Indian phenomena, this tradition is more closely associated with one cricketing city.

India's inaugural Test, at Lord's in June 1932, was played without Vijay Merchant, who had withdrawn from the England tour on account of his support for the ongoing civil disobedience movement. However, from the time Merchant made his international debut, in the Bombay Test against D.R. Jardine's visiting English team of 1933–4, Indian cricket has been serenely guided by the Bombay School of Batsmanship. Keeping the hundreds of millions of cricket-crazy Indians in mind, and following a famous British statesman, one might well say: 'Never in cricket history has so much been owed by so many to so few.'

The Australian wicket-keeper Wally Grout is believed to have said that when he saw Ken Barrington walking out to bat in an Ashes Test, he 'could see the Union Jack waving behind him.' Likewise, with the loss of early Indian wickets in a Test match, the arrival of a Bombay batsman at the crease has tended to make the tricolour move up abruptly from half mast.

This is not at all to claim that other cricketing centres have not produced great batsmen. In fact, no Bombay batsman—not even Gavaskar Mark II—has quite evoked the sense of anticipation on the arrival at the crease of C.K. Nayudu and Syed Mushtaq Ali (Holkar), Salim Durrani (Rajasthan), G.R. Viswanath (Karnataka), Krishnamachari Srikkanth (Tamil Nadu), Kapil Dev (Haryana) or Mohammed Azharuddin (Hyderabad). For enjoyment and entertainment, one could very well look elsewhere, but if one were to choose a man to bat for one's life (or save a Test match) one can turn only to Bombay. I can think quickly of only three Indian batsmen from outside the island city who, as they walked down the pavilion steps at the fall of a wicket, have provided the comforting confidence so often sought by the Indian spectator. These are Vijay Hazare and Chandu Borde, both Maharashtrians who came to cricketing maturity while playing at Bombay's twin city, Pune, and that modest but heroic Punjabi, Mohinder Amarnath.

The hallmarks of the Bombay School of Batsmanship are well acknowledged: immense concentration, resolute defence, rare courage, sharp cricketing acumen, nerves of steel, and—undergirding it all—a fierce pride in their cricketing heritage. Like all great traditions, however, this one too has allowed for considerable innovation: many subtle individual variations in style, built on a shared set of learned techniques.

I myself like to think of Bombay batsmen as pairs of spiritual 'masters and disciples'. Just as Merchant was Gavaskar's unacknowledged guru and alter ego, Sanjay Manjrekar carries on the tradition not of his father Vijay but of Rusi Modi, the tall, slim Parsi who likewise relied more on persuasion than on power, on the deflection and glide rather than on firm strokes in front of the wicket. It is only in the manner of playing the square cut—with a straight bat, following a body swivel towards the off side—that the son truly resembles the father. For the rest, Vijay Manjrekar was more classical in approach, a fine driver of the ball and (unlike Sanjay) a superb player of slow bowling. The senior Manjrekar's own mantle passed directly on to Dilip Sardesai, who resembles him in his stocky build, his equal command over spin and pace (he opened successfully for India), his ability through temperament and technique to successfully master a variety of situations (thus both had fine records overseas), and, though perhaps only incidentally, in his supreme indifference to fielding.

With Modi and Manjrekar, the third great representative of the Bombay School in the immediate post-Merchant phase was Polly Umrigar. Apart from his skills with the bat, Umrigar was also a fine off-break bowler and a brilliant slip, with capacious and sure hands. Although he lacked Polly's all-round versatility, Dilip Vengsarkar has resembled him in the power with which he played his strokes, and in the willingness, rare in Bombay batsmen, to loft the ball. (On Gary Sobers' first-class debut, as a sixteen-year-old slow left-arm bowler for Barbados against a visiting Indian side, Umrigar hit him more than once out of the Kennington Oval in Bridgetown—an assault the greatest of all cricketers has recalled with feeling in his autobiography.) We can likewise think of pairing Madhav Apte and Ravi Shastri, opening batsmen who played within their limitations, sold their wickets dearly, and (unlike many of their contemporaries) enjoyed an exceptional record against West Indian fast bowlers. Finally, one might consider Ajit Wadekar's baton being handed over to Vinod Kambli, another dashing, unorthodox left-hander whose exuberance was quickly tempered by the demands of Test cricket.

VI

Modi and Manjrekar (jr.), Manjrekar (sr.) and Sardesai, Umrigar and Vengsarkar, Apte and Shastri, Wadekar and Kambli. How lightly the names trip off the tongue, reminding us that despite their undoubted greatness, Vijay Merchant and Sunil Gavaskar are but two towering peaks in a range of mighty mountains that lies between them—and beyond. It is a tradition of which all India is proud, but which must put an enormous burden on its practitioners. Men like Viswanath or Azharuddin have played only for India; but when one of the Manjrekars (say) has gone out to bat at 10 for 2 in the first hour of a Test match, they have known it is their city's as much as their country's honour which is at stake.

And so, before he had turned seventeen, Sachin Tendulkar was being told—lest he become conceited before his time—'You'll never be as good as Gavaskar.' It is too early to pass judgement on Tendulkar, but I do wish now to pay tribute to another master of the Bombay School, to whom cricket writers and Indian spectators have done scant justice. For despite his magnificent record—over 7,000 Test runs, including three successive hundreds at Lord's (in the Tests of 1979, 1982 and 1986)—Dilip Vengsarkar was, in his early career, overshadowed in the public imagination by the presence of Sunil Gavaskar and, in his later years in Test cricket, by the emergence of the second acknowledged superstar of Indian cricket, Kapil Dev.

Suresh Menon of the *Indian Express* once penetratingly remarked that were David Gower born an Indian, and Dilip Vengsarkar an Englishman, they might have been more properly honoured for their achievements. Gower was both an extraordinarily gifted batsman and a man who visibly enjoyed his cricket—two besetting sins in the eyes of the English, who like their batsmen to be dour in countenance and safe rather than spectacular in their strokeplay. Where Indian cricket followers might have more readily recognized Gower, the man and the batsman, they never quite warmed to Vengsarkar. They have mistaken his reserve for lack of charm, for, unlike the English, Indians cannot understand men who are relentlessly focused on their craft (as Vengsarkar was), apparently lacking human contact and the human touch. But while some Indians might wish Vengsarkar to be reborn in Yorkshire, I am happy enough that he was born, in my time, in Bombay.

In an earlier study, I perhaps incautiously drew the following homology: Sunil Gavaskar is to Ravi Shankar as Gundappa Viswanath is to that other great sitar player, Vilayat

Khan. Some people protested strongly, and a former teacher of mine even wrote, in red pencil on the typed manuscript: 'The tone of comparison is *off*.' But I was reassured when a friend who, *pace* Neville Cardus, knows his music as well as his cricket in fact urged me to extend the comparison. 'If you wish to think of Ravi Shankar as Gavaskar and Vilayat Khan as Viswanath,' he remarked, 'why not think of Nikhil Bannerjee as Dilip Vengsarkar?'

I seized on this immediately. Just as Nikhil Bannerjee—who was perhaps ten years younger than the other two sitar wizards—took his early training under Ravi Shankar, Dilip Vengsarkar, almost inevitably, was deeply influenced in his formative years by Sunil Gavaskar. However, in common with Bannerjee, Vengsarkar in time came out of the master's shadow to develop an independent career and distinctive style of play. Ironically, like the Bombay batsman Bannerjee perhaps never quite got his just desserts, in part owing to his early death.

The comparison is apposite for a larger reason. For the Bombay School of Batsmanship might reasonably be compared to a muscial school or *gharana,* also usually associated with a particular city. Here too tradition and technique are passed down directly from master to disciple (what is called the *guru-shishya parampara*), allowing always for improvisation—and occasionally, forgetting—by the younger generation. In this tradition the master asks the highest standards of the apprentice, but will be fiercely protective of him in the presence of outsiders. On Gavaskar's first overseas tour, in the West Indies in 1971, the youngster was painfully shy at parties, sipping his soft drinks and refusing to be drawn out by his hosts. A Caribbean cricketer commented sarcastically on his reticence. He was at once set upon by Dilip Sardesai, who told him, 'You just watch out, before the tour is over our boy will have hit a double century against your team' (he did, with three single hundreds to boot). In the fullness of time Gavaskar was to provide this kind of

encouragement to Bombay batsmen younger than him, Dilip
Vengsarkar above all.

I first heard of cricket's Nikhil Bannerjee from two of my
college mates, Praveen Oberoi and Rajeshwar Vats, who in the
winter of 1974–5 had gone to the southern town of Mysore to
spearhead (or so we all thought) Delhi University to its then
customary victory in the finals of the All-India Inter-University
tournament for the Rohinton Baria Trophy. Oberoi bowled slow
left-arm, Vats right-arm fast-medium; they were accustomed to
easily defeating (and, in the latter's case, terrorizing) college and
university batsmen—both went on to have long first-class
careers. But on the Maharaja's College ground, with its red
sandy outfield I would hate to spend a day running about on,
they were given the thrashing of a lifetime by a lanky
wicket-keeper-batsman (for that is what he then was) named
Dilip Vengsarkar.

Vengsarkar came to wider public notice early the next
season. Making his first-class debut for Bombay against the Rest
of India, he hit a brilliant 110, including six sixes, off an attack
that included Bishen Bedi and Erapalli Prasanna. This innings,
which took the batsman straight into the Indian team, was played
at Nagpur, the birthplace of Colonel C.K. Nayudu, and
Vengsarkar was promptly nicknamed 'Colonel'.

The appellation stuck, but Bombay coaches and Sunil
Gavaskar worked relentlessly at reorienting his attitude and style
of batsmanship to the demands of international cricket. Under
their influence, for a while Vengsarkar, at least when playing for
India, became excessively cautious. Slowly the attacking
instincts reasserted themselves, although he never quite
recaptured the dash and abandon of his early youth.

At his best Vengsarkar was an imperious player. By some
distance the tallest of the great Indian batsmen at six feet one
inch, he stood up straight and stroked magnificently through the
off side off both back foot and front. Like almost all his

countrymen he played beautifully off his legs, although he rarely cut and, in common with some other tall men, was never really comfortable while hooking. He liked to start slowly, but could accelerate very quickly indeed; he was to play quite a few matchwinning innings in the limited overs game. In full flow he was a thrilling sight, uniquely combining both elegance and power.

I have watched some fine Vengsarkar innings both on the box and from the stands, but curiously the two knocks that stand out in my memory came to me, as it were, by hearsay. The first I have already alluded to, the 170 at Mysore which I heard described, with feeling, by Praveen Oberoi and Rajeshwar Vats. The second came to me while it happened, courtesy the All India Radio.

This innings was played in the second Test, played at Delhi, of the 1979–80 home series against Pakistan. The visitors batted first and scored 273, with that lazy, languid left-hander Wasim Raja (one of my favourite cricketers) hitting a strokeful ninety-seven. This total was made to look disproportionately large when Sikandar Bakht, an eager young colt making his first overseas tour, bowled India out for 126. (Bakht, who took 8 for 69 with sharp inswing, and Raja were both immediately sent specially struck gold medals on the rest day of the Test by the then President of Pakistan, General Zia-ul-Haq.) Fifties by Zaheer Abbas and Raja, again, took the Pakistan second innings to 242, an overall lead of 389.

India went in to bat midway through the fourth day, with eight hours to save the match or (not that very many people thought it likely) 390 runs to score to win it. Gavaskar left early, caught behind off Sikandar. Now defeat loomed large, a prospect made all the more depressing by General Zia's flamboyant and widely publicized gesture. The prestige of an entire nation rested on a few batsmen. The tension in the Indian dressing room must have been unbearable, though the absence of Imran Khan (through injury) offered some hope.

Vengsarkar came in to bat at number three. Through that long fourth afternoon and the almost interminable fifth day, he was kept company for the most part by two doughty but unsung heroes of Indian cricket's coming of age, Chetan Chauhan and Yashpal Sharma. Vengsarkar himself was sure but watchful, for like everyone else he had the dread of defeat uppermost in his mind.

But slowly the Pakistan attack tired, and the terrier-like Yashpal was urging his partner to run short singles. Vengsarkar's own drives began to flow, and suddenly the chase was on. Huddled over a radio two thousand miles away in Bangalore, I remember most vividly of all the description of a huge, towering cover drive Vengsarkar hit off the slow left-armer Iqbal Qasim. Now India began surging towards what would have been a truly extraordinary win. Then Yashpal fell, and so did Kapil Dev, after a quick twenty-one. Again Vengsarkar had no option but to play for a draw. India finally ended at 364 for six, 26 runs short of victory, with Dilip Vengsarkar 146 not out.

In his retirement Vengsarkar must look back with satisfaction on a playing career of considerable achievement: including a record at the home of cricket unmatched by any other batsman, and six Test centuries against the West Indies. As he looks out from his balcony at the monsoon winds coming over the Arabian Sea, I dare say that memories of that long vigil at the Firozshah Kotla must give him as much pleasure as any other innings he played for India

VII

The Bombay School of Batsmanship is a magnificent overarching tradition under which nest numerous little traditions; little streams, so to speak, which both feed into and seek renewal from the mighty river. These little centres of

Bombay cricket have included colleges (Elphinstone, St. Xavier's, Ruia and Poddar), clubs (Shivaji Park, Dadar Union, the P.J. Hindu Gymkhana), companies (the State Bank of India, Mafatlals, Tatas), and even the odd school. When Vinod Kambli, Sachin Tendulkar and Praveen Amre went berserk in a recent Bombay Test, a banner in the Wankhede Stadium read, simply, 'Shardashram versus England'. The reference was to a high school in central Bombay where all three had learnt to bat, under the coach of coaches, Ramakant Achrekar.

Before Tendulkar and Kambli were born, another Bombay school had indelibly stamped its mark on the history of Indian cricket. This was King George's School in Dadar (since renamed Raja Shivaji School), whose products have included that superb stumper, N.S. Tamhane, the graceful stylist Ramnath Kenny, and two of the greatest Bombay batsmen.

One of these is Dilip Vengsarkar, to whom we have already doffed our hats. The other is the late Vijay Manjrekar, a technician of the highest calibre whom I like to think of as the Bombay batsman's batsman. For he was the first authentic product of the city's dominant community, the first among the dozens of Maharashtrians who have since made cricketing prowess the vehicle for advancing high in the social hierarchy. The Bombay school had actually been founded by prosperous Gujaratis and Parsis (Merchant and Modi, for instance); but from Manjrekar onwards, it has been consolidated and carried forward by middle-class, Marathi-speaking boys from the densely packed localities of Dadar, Matunga and Shivaji Park.

Indeed, through example and precept Manjrekar was to closely guide a generation of Bombay batsmen. In his autobiography, *My Cricketing Years* Ajit Wadekar wrote that 'no Bombay cricketer, who has made the grade in recent times, will deny the debt he owes Vijay Manjrekar for his help, encouragement and guidance.' 'This great Indian batsman,' he continued, 'has been quick to spot and appreciate potential talent. Where some of his contemporaries were inclined to scoff at the abilities and dampen the enthusiasm of younger players, Manjrekar used to seek them out, point out the flaws in their technique, and then show how to correct them.'

When Wadekar was unexpectedly appointed captain for India's 1971 tour of the West Indies, it was Manjrekar who (probably at the skipper's suggestion) was asked to supervise the pre-tour nets at the Brabourne Stadium. The preparations must have been immaculate, for it was two Bombay batsmen who between themselves guided India to one win and four draws in the Caribbean—Sunil Gavaskar, of course, and Dilip Sardesai, the cricketer who has most resembled Manjrekar in his approach to the game.

Manjrekar himself was born with cricket in his blood, for his maternal uncle was the dapper D.D. Hindlekar, the Indian wicket-keeper on the 1936 and 1946 tours of England. In fact he started off as a wicket-keeper himself, and even kept wickets in a Test match in the West Indies. As a batsman, which is how we remember him, Manjrekar possessed a marvellous technique and strokes all round the wicket. Both traits were in evidence in his first Test innings in England, played in the summer of 1952. On a seaming wicket at Headlingley, he went in to bat with the score reading 42 for 3. Composed and assured from the start, he hit fifteen crisp boundaries in a chanceless hundred, against an attack led by Freddie Trueman and Alec Bedser.

Among Manjrekar's array of shots, the hook, the cover drive and the cut stood out. When India played Australia at Madras in October 1956, Keith Miller, one half of a feared fast bowling combination, was sitting out the match, injured. After Manjrekar had gone in to bat, with India at 44 for 2, he twice cut Ray Lindwall down to the pavilion for four. On seeing these boundaries Miller turned to his neighbour, S.K. Gurunathan of *The Hindu*, and remarked, 'Those were beautiful strokes. I wish I were bowling to him.'

On his second tour of England, in 1959, Manjrekar was plagued with a knee injury. He was rarely at his best, one exception being the match against the Champion County, Surrey. In an innings of 183, he picked Jim Laker's floater time and again, cutting it for four. The off-spinner V.M. Muddiah, who described this innings to me thirty years later, called Manjrekar the finest all-round batsman he had seen or played with, a master on any wicket and against any kind of bowling. When bowling to Manjrekar, he recalled, you sometimes felt totally helpless, sending down six balls merely as a formality to complete an over.

Muddiah's despair was shared by other opponents, on the field, of Manjrekar. One such was the England captain, Ted Dexter. On a tour of India, in the winter of 1961–2, his side came up against the Bombay batsman at his most commanding. Manjrekar scored 583 runs in a series which India won by two Tests to nil, but it was not so much the number of runs as the manner of their making which Dexter remembered. Till he saw Manjrekar, he wrote later, 'I had never appreciated the extent to which a batsman could be in total—and I mean *total*—control of what he is doing and of everything the bowler was trying to do with him.' This was a rare compliment, for only the previous winter Dexter had toured in the West Indies, where he had spent many hours in the field chasing hits by Sobers, Kanhai and Worrell. The Englishman recalled, with reverence and as an illustration of Manjrekar's command, the ease with which he would pinch a single off the last ball of an over—regardless of the bowling or the field Dexter set to stop him. In fact, this ability frustrated his fellow batsmen as much as it did his opponents. One who played Test cricket with Manjrekar remembered him as a '*pukka chor*', who revelled in stealing the strike.

All Bombay cricketers play the game hard, but Manjrekar played it harder than most. He was also a most laconic character. On that 1952 tour of England, India played a mid-season match against Sussex. While batting, Manjrekar went for a mighty pull to a short off-break. He missed the ball, but in his follow through knocked down the wicket-keeper with his bat. The man thus felled was Billy Griffith, later to be Secretary of the MCC. As Griffith got up, his mouth bleeding, Manjrekar is supposed to have told him, 'You are my fourth victim for the season.'

My favourite Manjrekar story appears in Rajan Bala's recent book on B.S. Chandrasekhar. In a Ranji Trophy match between Mysore and Rajasthan for whom Manjrekar played as a professional, Chandrasekhar bowled the maestro a fast googly. Pitched six inches outside the off stump, and on a perfect length, the ball swiftly darted in to take the off stump. Or so the bowler thought, but as his arms went up in triumph, Manjrekar's bat had intercepted the ball's progress, chopping it late to the third man boundary. Arrogant as ever, he strolled down to the bowler's end, patted Chandrasekhar on the butt and remarked, 'Good ball. But not good enough for Vijay Manjrekar.' Recounting that incident, Chandra observed that bowling to Manjerkar was like bowling to a wall—a remark that could have popped out of the mouth of Malcolm Marshall, apropos of Sunil Gavaskar, or of Alec Bedser, with regard to Vijay Merchant. (In fact, after Gavaskar's great debut series in the Caribbean, a Trinidad songster composed a calypso which ran, 'He's just like a wall, a wall/We can't get him out at all.')

I especially like this story of Chandrasekhar's early encounter with Manjrekar for its illustration of the clash between Indian cricket's two Great Traditions. For Indian Test teams, of course, spin bowling and Bombay batsmanship have worked magnificently in tandem. But in domestic cricket, where the two traditions have frequently come up against one another, it is invariably spin bowling that has had to give way—if only in confirmation of the bitter truth that this game is meant mainly for batsmen.

CHAPTER SIX

The Best-Loved Cricketer

W hen the Kalka Mail steamed into Delhi station that winter evening, exactly twelve years ago as I write, cricket was not on my mind. I probably knew, vaguely, that there was a Test match on in the capital, but I had not come from Calcutta to bask in the sun at the Firozshah Kotla. I was in fact in search of manuscripts that I hoped were still preserved in the dark recesses of the National Archives of India.

The two years since I had left Sunil Gavaskar 92 not out at Chepauk had been crowded but, astonishingly in view of my earlier life, quite free of cricket. I had made steady progress on my doctoral dissertation and, while living in the home of the longest serving *elected* communist government in the world, towards mastering the language and technical apparatus of Marxism. Marxists have tended to believe that sport is a bourgeois conspiracy to keep the workers from revolting, a theory which even C.L.R. James' mentor, Leon Trotsky, refused to be shaken from. But where in the Caribbean (as James was to famously demonstrate) cricket had served as a vehicle for racial and national emancipation, in India it had never pretended to be other than a form of entertainment. Thus the more Marxist I became in Calcutta, the more I left cricket behind. The ultimate step I took in this regard was to give away my library of cricket books, both as a mark of renunciation and to make room on my shelves for the texts of my new-found commitments.

When I reached my uncle's house from the train station, it was empty. The cook informed me that the whole family, except the sixteen-year-old son, had gone to Bombay on holiday. The boy came in a little while after me, his face flushed with more than the winter sun. 'I'm just back from the Test,' he exclaimed in excitement—for he knew me only as an elder cousin who was (or had been when we last met) cricket mad—'and Vishy is still batting on sixty.' India were playing England at the Firozshah Kotla, and G.R. Viswanath was 60 not out.

II

It had been a difficult year for G.R. Viswanath. He had done little of note with the bat in the two previous Tests of the series, and his fielding had steadily deteriorated. For the first time in a twelve-year career at the top, his place in the Indian side was being questioned, and prior to the Delhi Test there had arisen a strong movement among officials and journalists, pressing for his exclusion. The little man was himself worried enough to make a journey to the holy shrine at Tirupathi, praying for good fortune. He finally did play at Delhi, but only at the insistence of the captain, Sunil Gavaskar. Now here he was at the end of the second day, undefeated with 60 runs against his name.

The next morning my cousin made his way to the Kotla. But I did not go as planned to the National Archives, swayed both by the boy's excitement and by the prospect of seeing, if only on the television, its object. When play began Vishy kept his strokes firmly under check; for he knew only a century would silence his critics. Playing the spinners from the crease and gliding and deflecting the faster bowlers, he calmly reached 97, having hit only one boundary all morning. Then Derek Underwood pitched one ball a little short, and the trademark square cut brought up Vishy's hundred. A huge cheer went up around the ground, most certainly joined in by the millions of Indians listening in on the radio or watching on the box.

After lunch I departed finally for the archives, but the spirit had been rekindled. It was some time before Marxism completely gave way to a former love, and I am still rebuilding my cricket library (as well as trying to sell off my other one—there are few buyers in 1994 for ninety volumes of Lenin). I have often wondered, however, had it not been Viswanath but some other Indian batsman, would the homecoming have been as swift or painless?

After that innings in Delhi, Viswanath went on to score a flawless 222 in the next Test at Madras, when he and Yashpal Sharma batted for more than a day to the disgust, and utter frustration, of Ian Botham. Frank Keating wrote of this double hundred that it combined 'utter grandeur' (the batsmanship) with 'almost sheepish modesty' (the man). But as it happened, Vishy's career had not much longer to run. The following winter in Pakistan saw him, in common with the other Indian batsmen (Gavaskar and Mohinder Amarnath only excepted), being sorted out by Imran Khan. Most of his admirers associate the end of Viswanath with an Imran inswinger that bowled him for a first-ball duck at Karachi, late on the afternoon of Christmas Day, 1982. However at Gavaskar's insistence again (and so that he would break the record for the most consecutive appearances in Test cricket), he was to play two more matches in the series.

In the first of these matches, at Hyderabad, Viswanath did show a tantalizingly brief glimpse of his genius. Already two down in the series, India were shot out for 189 replying to Pakistan's mammoth score of 581 for 3 declared (Viswanath went again for zero, leg-before-wicket to Imran). Following on, India quickly lost two wickets. Thus Vishy went in to bat late on the fourth day, with a match and career to salvage. He looked in as good form as he had been for some time. A sequence of crisp cuts and drives, mostly through the off side, took him to 35 not out at the close. This time I needed little prodding to be in front of the box at ten-thirty the next morning.

When play began on the final day of the Test Vishy was at the non-striker's end. Dilip Vengsarkar took a single to fine leg off the first ball. On reaching the batting crease the maestro tugged at his cap and, with bat held firm and upright on the turf, briskly skipped up and down on the wicket. It was a gesture I recognized immediately; it meant that Vishy, otherwise so languid in his movements, was priming himself for action—the equivalent, shall we say, of an expressive tennis player in a moment of crisis slapping his backside, clenching his fists, and muttering to himself: 'Come on, come on!' It promised much. Then Sarfraz Nawaz bowled an inswinger moving down the leg side. Vishy made to glance, missed the ball, and was struck on the pads at least six inches outside the leg stump. The bowler appealed, and Vishy, who at this stage stood between the home side and victory (Gavaskar and Amarnath were already in the pavilion) was adjudged leg-before. He departed immediately, but not before giving a hard, and for him unprecedented, look at the man who gave him out. Not for the last time was a great cricketing career undone by a Pakistani umpire.

III

If cricket, as the writer Geoffrey Moorhouse once put it, is the best-loved game, then G.R. Viswanath was surely the best-loved cricketer. Writing of the events leading up to that Delhi Test of 1982 in his book *Cricket Wallah*, Scyld Berry observed: 'If you love Viswanath—and most of India does . . .'

I have loved him more than most, for what are intensely personal reasons. We share a hometown and what's more, Viswanath was the first Test cricketer I ever shook hands with.

In the summer of 1970, my uncle Durai and I were driving alongside Bangalore's magnificent Cubbon Park when, on Nrupatunga Road near the city's YMCA, he spied a diminutive, but for him familiar figure hunched low over a motor scooter. A yell and a wave brought the man to a halt, and soon greetings and handshakes were being exchanged with the shy, smiling hero of the previous winter's Kanpur Test against the Australians.

Durai himself claims that he was in some small way responsible for the rise of Viswanath. A vocal member of the Karnataka State Cricket Association, with some other loud shouting men he dismissed with derision a statement by a selector of the state junior team that Viswanath was 'too short' to play representative cricket. The rebuke went home, for Vishy was finally selected, scored a hundred and, on his subsequent elevation to the Karnataka Ranji Trophy side, an unbeaten double century on debut. The next season he was playing Test cricket.

Whatever the truth of Durai's claim, I have always felt somewhat proprietorial about Viswanath. And so, indeed, does everyone else in our hometown. The last time I saw him play was in late 1988, in the finals of a city tournament. His side, the State Bank of India, were playing their old enemy, the State Bank of Mysore. Vishy scored twenty odd when his team batted first, an innings that gave great joy to the small crowd. When the State Bank of India took the field, he very soon took a sharp catch at first slip off the bowling of Roger Binny. Binny raced down the length of the pitch, but was narrowly beaten in his attempt to hug Vishy by their teammate for club, state and country, Syed Kirmani. Both bowler and wicket-keeper were delighted for the little man.

But of course, Viswanath does not belong to Bangalore alone. From Mansur Ali Khan Pataudi to Kapil Dev, Indian Test cricketers who played alongside him have claimed him as their favourite colleague. And he has also been the best loved of opponents. I have written elsewhere of Greg Chappell's affectionate but wholly untypical acclaim as fielding captain when Vishy scored a hundred in a low-scoring Melbourne Test, and on a better-known occasion the England all-rounder Tony Greig picked him up when he reached the same milestone, to the delight of a full house at the Brabourne Stadium. But it has not needed a long innings for foreign cricketers, or commentators, to express their appreciation of the man. I can hear as I write the warmth of Trevor Bailey's commendation, when he made a short, strokeful fifteen in India's great, unavailing bid to win the 1979 Oval Test, of 'Little Vishy's *cameo* of an innings.'

This universal love, in an age where international cricket is marked by bitter national rivalry and the clash of personalities, is truly remarkable. It has something to do with his character, which is quietly dignified, and above all, true. It has also something to do with his stature, for as the giant Tony Greig's cradling of Viswanath in the Bombay Test of 1973 so well symbolized, it was a wonder how such a little man could do so much. And it has something to do with the quality of his batsmanship, to which we must now briefly return.

If one were to subject a cricket watcher of the Nineteen Seventies to a stroke-association test, to 'G.R. Viswanath' he would immediately reply: 'Square cut!' That shot was indeed his peculiar glory, and he played it with rare power and ease of placement. In my admiration for the craft of Bishen Bedi, I once claimed that the slow left-arm bowler was never cut, to which a friend responded, 'Yes, he was! Ranji quarter-final, Bangalore, 1974. By G.R.' It was a match we had both watched, and the reminder was salutary. In an innings of 65 (run out) Viswanath—a tiny, crouching figure moving quickly about the crease—repeatedly made room to square and late cut good length spinning deliveries for four. (Backward point had a hell of a time, running yards one way and then the other, mostly in vain. It was an experience he was still talking about when I joined his college in Delhi the following year.) Among other spin bowlers, Abdul Qadir and Derek Underwood both have good reason to remember the Viswanath square cut. It was a stroke he played with relish against the quicker bowlers too. Where to spinners he caressed rather than forced the ball, usually playing it behind square, to the fast stuff he stood upright and hit the ball fiercely past point.

But Beethoven is much more than the Fifth Symphony, and great batsmen cannot, even in the popular imagination, be reduced to one stroke. Next on Vishy's own repertoire was the square drive, a shot closely allied to the square cut. This was played off the front foot, with knees bent, and usually off the pace bowlers. On the on side, Vishy played with facility that distinctively Indian stroke, the wristy flick off the toes, as well as a paddle sweep more lately associated with Mohammed Azharuddin. All these shots he was master of till the end of his playing days, but those fortunate to have watched him in his prime will remember too his majestic on drive and the whip through midwicket also played by Dilip Vengsarkar, albeit with more power.

Vishy was at his best as a batsman from about 1972 to 1975. Thereafter, his fondness for beer and lack of physical discipline—here he was in sharp contrast to the abstemious Gavaskar—reduced his mobility and dimmed his reflexes. Towards the end of his career he came to rely very much on the square cut and square drive, and on the leg side placement; a repertoire thin by his own exalted standards, but ample enough to get him those two successive hundreds against Keith Fletcher's England side of 1981–2.

Curiously though, one strokemaking innovation he left till very late. Watching him at the nets in Bangalore, I often saw him clout his side's spin bowlers (Prasanna and Chandrasekhar, no less) onto the roof of the Chinnaswamy Stadium, but in first-class matches he virtually never lifted the ball. My first memory of him doing so on the field of play is in the 1976 series, during the second Port of Spain Test. At about two in the morning, a group of us were crowded round a radio in the college quadrangle, listening to the middle stages of India's heroic bid for victory against the West Indies (they had been set more than four hundred in the fourth innings). At a key moment, Vishy hit the left-arm slow bowler, Rafique Jumadeen, over mid-off for four. We exchanged glances, for this was new. Clive Lloyd dropped mid-off further back, but Vishy cleared him again. He went on to get a hundred, and India won in a canter.

I also remember Vishy hitting two lofted straight drives off Phil Edmonds in that 'little cameo' he played in the last hour of the 1979 Oval Test against England. Turning to a less well-known occasion, I once watched Vishy, at the Firozshah Kotla, in a Ranji Trophy match between Karnataka and Delhi, being beaten on the back foot by a delivery from the rising university star, Praveen Oberoi. The ball had come in late with the arm instead of, as the batsman had anticipated, spinning away towards the off side. The ball was only narrowly missing leg stump, and the bowler, after pleading with the umpire to give the decision in his favour, sank to the ground in despair. At the end of the over Oberoi made a great show to his teammates of what he felt was a case of justice denied. Vishy watched calmly, but at the beginning of Oberoi's next over, came dancing down the wicket to send the ball into the crowd over extra-cover.

Even the gentlest of men are sometimes moved to show an upstart his place.

IV

In a long and distinguished career, G. R. Viswanath hit hundreds against Michael Holding at Port of Spain, Imran Khan at Faisalabad, Ian Botham at Lord's, and Denis Lillee at

Melbourne. Those centuries are all part of Indian cricket history; two of them won Test matches, the two others saved them. More warmly remembered by his countrymen, however, are innings played by Vishy at home. As if in acknowledgement of his best-loved status, the little man has showered his gifts abundantly on the cricket centres of India. Every Indian Test ground, it appears, has a great Viswanath innings associated with it. Kanpur can claim his first, matchsaving hundred against the Australians in 1969, 137 not out with twenty-five glittering boundaries; Bombay can hold up his 123 against England three years later, when he emphatically broke the voodoo that had till then surrounded all previous Indian batsmen who would score a hundred on Test debut only to fail at every subsequent attempt to reach the magic figure; and Delhi is still fiercely possessive of the century hit against Underwood and company in December 1981, the knock with which I began this chapter. His hometown, Bangalore, has of course much else to remember him by, but he was thoughtful enough to score at least one Test hundred at the Chinnaswamy Stadium, against Kim Hughes' Australian side of 1979.

But Vishy's greatest innings at home were saved up for Calcutta and Madras, perhaps the two most discriminating of cricket centres. These were, in fact, played in successive Tests of the series of 1974–5, in which India came up against a formidable West Indian side led by Clive Lloyd. The home team had started the series in the lowest of spirits, having lost all the Tests on the previous summer's tour of England. For this home series they had retained much the same side, although Pataudi had replaced Ajit Wadekar as captain. On the eve of the first Test against the West Indies (played at Bangalore), Vijay Merchant delivered a stinging rebuke to the Indian batsmen, Viswanath most of all. 'During our many Test matches in India and abroad,' wrote Merchant, 'time and again our batsmen make their thirties and forties but rarely go on to make a big score.

91

Viswanath is a glaring example. Why do our batsmen settle down only to get out soon afterwards?'

The first of the great Indian batsmen ascribed this deficiency to lack of concentration, lack of stamina and lack of teamwork.[*] It is most unlikely that Viswanath came across this essay though, knowing Merchant, he might very well have chastised him in person too. In any case, Vishy's recent performances bore testimony to the truth of Merchant's remarks. In the three Test matches on the 1974 tour of England, his scores had been 40 and 50, 52 and 5, 28 and 25—five times out of six, getting set only to get out. The trend continued in the first two Tests against Clive Lloyd's side, Vishy scoring 29 and 22 at Bangalore and 32 and 39 at Delhi, India losing the first of these matches by 267 runs, the second by an innings and seventeen. I watched the last of these knocks, an exquisite cameo of cuts and on drives, brought to an end by a spectacular catch by Clive Lloyd, diving in front of him at midwicket, after Vishy had mistimed a drive off Lance Gibbs.

And so India arrived in Calcutta having lost the first two Tests by huge margins, and in the knowledge that Sunil Gavaskar would be out through injury for the next two. At the Eden Gardens India batted first, then conceded a first innings lead of seven runs. When they batted again two wickets fell early, in an all too familiar pattern. Now Viswanath joined Engineer in a partnership of restoration. After Farokh left, Vishy saw three others come and go before the left-handed all-rounder, Karsan Ghavri, in his first Test, bravely pitched camp. Ghavri kept the ball out as Viswanath with a series of cuts, glides and drives reached an immaculate century. Thus India were able to cross three hundred, setting a target on a turning wicket that was beyond the reach of the West Indies.

---

[*] Vijay Merchant, 'We are the Champion Nation (in Making Excuses)', in Suresh Saraiya, editor, *West Indies in India, 1974–5* (Neeta Publications, 1974).

The two teams then moved on to Madras. Here India chose, perhaps unwisely, to bat first on a spiteful wicket, fast and of unpredictable bounce. Against the menacing Andy Roberts a total under a hundred seemed a distinct possibility, but Vishy rose to the challenge. While Roberts carved through the rest of the Indians, the little man subjected the fastest bowler in the world to a fierce beating (Roberts' final figures, of 7 wickets for 64 runs in a mere twenty overs, tell this story of his dominance of ten men and his defeat by one). The journalist Partab Ramchand, who covered the match, later wrote of two shots that were to be forever impressed on his memory: a hook and an on drive that passed Roberts on his follow through. But the Doordarshan cameraman evidently had other favourites, for in the highlights of the innings—which I watched in Delhi the next day, the live television coverage being restricted to the city of the Test—he had singled out for special attention two off side shots. Both were square drives played off the front foot which neatly pierced two quick movers on the boundary edge, Keith Boyce at deep third man and Vivian Richards at deep backward point. When he at last ran out of partners Viswanath had scored 97 not out. For the second time running, Vijay Merchant had got the answer he wished for. As in Calcutta, it was an innings without which India could not have won. Men who have watched cricket in Chepauk over fifty years tell me that this was most certainly the best innings played on that ground. Given the quality of the bowling and the state of the wicket, it was also most likely the finest innings played by an Indian on Indian soil.

V

From the beginning Viswanath and Gavaskar were doomed to comparison; both little men, whose careers overlapped for the most part, who between them carried the Indian batting for a decade, and who, to cap it all, were brothers-in-law in real life.

It is a comparison made the more inevitable by both cricketers' perfectly sincere insistence on the other man's superiority with the bat.

Indian cricket lovers have been known to come to blows on the question. But perhaps this is not as much a comparison as a contrast, for no two players could have been less alike in character or cricketing style. While there may be two opinions on who was, objectively speaking, the 'better batsman', any discussion would inevitably highlight the marked differences in technique, in range and manner of strokeplay and, not least, in personality.

Who might Vishy as a batsman then be compared with? Tom Alter, the film actor and cricketer of American origin, told me of a recent meeting with Alvin Kallicharan, where 'Kalli' proudly told him that he was born in the same year as Gavaskar and Viswanath (1949) and was also, at exactly five feet four inches, half an inch shorter than the one and threequarters of an inch shorter than the other. Although West Indian by temperament Kallicharan was, of course, Indian by origin. It is indeed possible to think of Kalli, a marvellous cutter and adept off his legs, as a sort of left-handed Viswanath, although only a Caribbean would be capable of handing out the kind of savage beating he subjected Denis Lillee to in an early match of the 1975 World Cup.

To return to strictly Indian parallels, I like to think of G.R. Viswanath as the centre-point of the *other* tradition of Indian batsmanship. This is the tradition of wristy batting stylists that goes back even further than the better known Bombay School, for it begins with K.S. Ranjitsinhji. An Indian cricket writer has recently assimilated Ranji's batting style to the struggle against imperialism, arguing that his famous leg-glance, played across the line, expressly cocked a snook at Victorian orthodoxy and by extension, at the Empire. Without going so far, one can nonetheless see a clear contrast between the line of stylists begun by Ranji and the Bombay School. Where Bombay batsmen could teach a lesson or two to the coaches of the Marylebone Cricket Club (it was, I think, C.B. Fry who referred to Vijay Merchant as 'India's Good European'), Ranji and his spiritual successors hardly played a Christian stroke, though they have played some distinctively Hindu and Islamic ones. No one has given, and indeed exuded, greater joy than the Indian stylist at the wicket. And it can be said with confidence, though perhaps not in Bombay, that the stylist has even won and saved the odd Test match.

It is in this tradition that Viswanath falls. C.B. Fry wrote of K.S. Ranjitsinhji, the tradition's founder so to speak, that unlike English batsmen with 'their ponderous movements' of hand and foot, Ranji had 'a more subtle and more supple manner of moving; he moves as if he had no bones.' Although much shorter than the prince of Nawanagar, Viswanath had much the same grace and economy of movement. In his batsmanship he followed Ranji's famous maxim, 'Play back or drive'—both eschewed that most ungainly and most common of shots, the forward defensive push with bat behind pad. And these words, taken from Ranji's *Jubilee Book of Cricket*, might have been written with Vishy in mind,

> [the] cut has this other great recommendation, that in order to make it the batsman need expend very little muscular effort; indeed, a batsman who is a master hand at cutting can score almost as fast as a very hard hitter without tiring himself a quarter as much.

Ranji's official biographer, Alan Ross, once wrote that the cut and the leg glide were the strokes which most distinguished the wristy stylist from the more orthodox, and more limited, batsman. This we might accept, but Ross also claimed (in the same essay) that the stylist was always tall and slim—thus 'figure and deportment are relevant to style, for it is hard to think of a squat batsman, however good, who qualifies.' He appears not to have seen Viswanath bat. But Ross' roster of great stylists did include three other Indians. One of these was S.Mushtaq Ali, a master of the cut and glide, and much else besides. R.S. Whittington, who played against Mushtaq Ali in 1945, called him India's 'modern Ranji'; the most natural of cricketers, with the footwork of a panther and a style of batting that 'was all flame; we were caught in the conflagration.'

Mushtaq Ali hit two hundreds and seven fifties in the eleven official Test matches he played; a record perhaps not commensurate with his exceptional gifts, yet one far superior to that of two other Indian batsmen also remembered for their elegance. These were C.D. Gopinath of Madras, a beautiful cutter of the ball, and Ramnath Kenny, who played for Bombay but came originally from the west coast of Karnataka—thus a man who combined in himself the best of two batting traditions. Kenny had but one half century in five Tests, Gopinath two in eleven. Abbas Ali Baig, another of this ilk, started more promisingly, hitting a dazzling hundred on debut at Manchester in 1959. The London *Times* wrote of Baig at the wicket that he 'glides like a cat burglar instead of attacking with the effrontery of a bandit'—words which capture perfectly the deftness with which the Indian stylist has taken apart bowling attacks.

Sadly, Baig's subsequent Test career went much the way of Gopinath's and Kenny's. It was left to G.R. Viswanath to redeem them all.

VI

I have saved up for the end the man who, of the long line of Indian stylists, has most resembled Viswanath in temperament and style of batsmanship. He was, of course, K.S. Duleepsinhji. What I have read about Duleep and seen of Vishy points to many areas of likeness: artful use of the crease, delightful wristwork (the Nawanagar man was also a master of the square and late cut) and a glorious unconcern for the record-books. An English cricket writer wrote of Duleep, much as others have since of Viswanath, that he 'charmed the ball away rather than hit it. There was no evidence of force, no aggression, simply perfection of timing, direction, control.'

Ironically, they also shared a common weakness, against quickish left arm spin. Viswanath was never entirely happy facing Derek Underwood and Iqbal Qasim, bowlers distinctly faster through the air than the classical left arm spinner such as Bedi; and Duleep was tormented by the tall Australian of this ilk, P.M. Hornibrook, who outside of the cricket field practiced dentistry in Brisbane. In the Ashes series of 1930, Hornibrook put the Indian sign on Duleep, dismissing him (usually caught or stumped down the leg side) eight times out of the twelve occasions they met. This prompted a journalist to comment, 'Duleep would rather go to Hornibrook to get a tooth extracted than face him bat in hand.'

Like Vishy too, Duleep was never known to leaf through the pages of *Wisden* in the dressing room or, while batting, to look up at the scoreboard. The writer Dudley Carew has written somewhere of congratulating Duleep on a brilliant hundred he had watched him score. Oh, replied Duleep modestly, that was certainly not one of his better innings. But had he seen the fourteen at Hove the previous week? Carew replied in the negative. Ah, went on the batsmen, that was an innings to be proud of. The leg glance he began with, recalled Duleep, rubbing his hands with relish. And the cover drive the next ball. *That* day he was in his element. What a shame gully got in the way of his square cut.

When he retired early through illness, a London newspaper called Duleep 'incomparably the best beloved of his period in English cricket.' Two Australian cricketers, otherwise sparing in their praise, have endorsed this. Don Bradman remembered

Duleep as 'not having an enemy in the world', while Victor Richardson (grandfather of Ian and Greg Chappell, and harder than both) said the Indian prince was without doubt 'the finest gentleman he had met on a cricket field.'*

The English themselves called him 'Tulip', a nickname that captures both the elegance of his batsmanship and the fragility of his physique. A charming story of his 'best loved' status among them comes from Duleep's great summer of 1930. This was the year he batted so brilliantly against Australia, scoring 416 runs, at an average of nearly sixty, in four Test matches. In the last of these, played at The Oval, the Indian journalist B. Shiva Rao was late coming to the ground. Play had been in progress an hour, but as Shiva Rao queued up for a ticket a boy selling scorecards spotted the Indian and said, 'Don't waste your money. Tulip is out and the rest [of the England batting] don't count.' They didn't, indeed.

The same summer, Duleep's uncle, a high Indian potentate and in his time the most famous of English cricketers, arrived late one night in a town in the north of England, without a place to stay. He went to a hotel, where he was told that all rooms were booked. 'But I am Ranji, K.S. Ranjitsinhji, the Jam Saheb of Nawanagar,' said the great man. 'I am sorry, sir,' replied the reception clerk, 'there are no rooms available.' In a flash of inspiration Ranji answered, 'But I am Duleep's uncle.' 'Why didn't you say so in the first place,' said the clerk with a smile, and showed him to the best suite in the hotel.

VII

There are some, nay many Indians, who will not allow G.R. Viswanath to be compared with anybody else. When Jack

---

* See Vijay Merchant, Vasant Raiji, Anandji Dossa and Vithalbhai Jhaveri, editors, *Duleep: the Man and His Game* (K.S. Duleepsinhji Commemoration Volume Committee, 1963).

Fingleton first began playing grade cricket in Sydney, he asked his club captain, the former Test wicket-keeper Hanson Carter, whether a contemporary Australian stylist reminded him of Victor Trumper. 'You must never,' replied Carter sternly, 'compare Vic with any other batsman. He was up there, all on his own.'

Carter obviously had both Trumper's batsmanship and nobility of character in mind. And so it has sometimes been with Viswanath, the best-loved cricketer, literally beyond compare.

CHAPTER SEVEN

Stumpers of Spin

> Wicket-keepers are like office-boys in at least one
> way—few people take notice of them until something gets
> in a mess, a folder or a chance is lost, an inkpot or a catch
> spilt, a mail or a stumping missed.

—*Ray Robinson*

Let us return to Mihir Bose's intriguing thesis on the
connections between a culture's alimentary techniques
and its preferences on the cricket field. A fellow cricket
writer, Suresh Menon, was so struck by this line of
argument that he sought to further extend its application. Where
Mihir Bose wished merely to explain the absence of good
left-handed batsmen, Suresh Menon daringly interpreted the
profusion of high-class wicket-keepers in India to be a
consequence of the traditional Indian 'squatting' style of
emptying the bowels. Crouching low with intense concentration
is the first act performed by Indians virtually every day of their
lives: lifelong preparation, in effect, for that most difficult job
in cricket, squatting behind the wickets.

To the Menon coda to the Bose theorem I now wish to add
a further caveat. It seems to me that while the Indian style of
pottying is, in general, the best training for those who choose in

later life to become stumpers, it is especially well suited for keeping wickets to slow bowlers. For the technique of wicket-keeping in this case requires one, when standing up to the stumps, to crouch lower and keep down longer than when keeping to fast bowlers from a dozen yards further back (when one is required to be poised somewhat higher, so as to get a better sight of the ball, as well as to rise faster, to take the higher bounce). 'The lower you get and the longer you stay down the better you will be' is a maxim all Indians are taught to respect from early childhood; it could well have been devised with keeping wicket to slow bowlers in mind.

Little wonder then that Indian stumpers have been so good while standing up to the wickets. The great spinners of the past, while sometimes lacking support from their fielders, were all exceptionally well-served by their wicket-keepers. On the 1911 tour of England, Palwankar Baloo had as his alter ego K. Seshachari, a high caste Iyengar from Madras who was the first South Indian to play representative cricket. Writing forty years before the publication of Mihir Bose's opus, and forty years after he had watched Seshachari play at the Eden Gardens, another Bengali writer penned this indelible description of India's first great wicket-keeper:

> I can recall from memory the figure of the cricket colossus, Seshachari, dark and forbidding, in his stand in close vicinity behind the stumps. The fastest ball would not remove him from his place of operation so near to the batsman's citadel. He crouched low and I wondered if the bails would not be dislodged from their cradle on top of the stumps by the volume of air let out by his lungs which I thought had the capacity of bellows. He reminded me of the sinister hill that hangs over the edge of a plain. I noticed some of his fingertips were somewhat crooked. What made them so? The question intrigues me even today![*]

---

[*] Romesh Ganguli, 'The Spirit of Cricket', in *Silver Jubilee Souvenir of the Cricket Association of Bengal* (Cricket Association of Bengal, 1954), p.53.

II

The Bose-Menon-Guha theorem would have greatly tickled the man who kept wickets when Indian cricket came of age. He is, and remains, a cricketer with a rich sense of humour. Farokh Engineer could in fact crouch as low as the next Indian, but he came up as quickly as a jack-in-the-box. He was a magnificent keeper to slow bowling, catching with equal facility the low off side snick off Bishen Bedi and the sharply rising inside edge off B.S. Chandrasekhar.

Engineer conducted a clutch of close catchers that gave the Holy Trinity such fine support in the field: Ajit Wadekar at slip, Venkatraghavan at silly point or in the gully, Abid Ali at leg slip, and the incomparable Eknath Solkar at short square leg. He led the murmurs of appreciation that accompanied every probing delivery and, full-throatedly, the chorus of appeals when a ball hit the pad or appeared to take an edge. Farokh, wrote a visiting English journalist in disgust after his side had lost a Test at the Eden Gardens, 'conducted a forty-five thousand strong choral society.'

Of the many adjectives in the English language that could and have been made to apply to Farokh, the one I most prefer is 'ebullient'. It alone captures in full the alacrity with which he would dive for a catch off a tentative edge, before it fell to the ground; or whip off the bails to effect a leg-side stumping; or, indeed, rise five feet in the air as his cohort Solkar made one of those astonishing catches at the batsman's feet. Alan Knott, himself the most orthodox and undemonstrative of wicket-keepers, was at the non-striker's end when Engineer caught John Edrich off the bowling of Bishen Bedi in the Lord's Test of 1971. Edrich played forward and got a thick edge, the ball hitting Farokh hard on the chest. As it fell to the ground, the wicket-keeper deftly flicked it up in the air with his left foot and completed the catch.

Though Knott was not to know it, this dexterous combination of hand and foot had its origins in Engineer's early sporting career, which was on the football rather than the cricket field. For Farokh had been a student at the Don Bosco School in Wadala, where the Irish Jesuit priests encouraged soccer as the main sport (they had an antipathy to cricket which might perhaps have had deep, anti-colonial origins). Thus Engineer first made his mark as an acrobatic goalkeeper—a training which lay behind both his obvious lack of technique (to quote an Australian writer, Engineer stood behind the stumps 'with his feet wider apart than any textbook suggests') and his marvellous improvising skills.

This ebullience spilled over into Farokh's batting—and it was a part of his personality outside of the cricket field too. John Woodcock, the cricket correspondent of the London *Times*, was once driven by Engineer to the Santa Cruz airport. He hung on for dear life, but on reaching England, was able to put Farokh's driving in perspective: 'He plays the way he drives . . . he drives as he bats, or bats as he drives, not always with due care and attention, with an eye for the gap and above all, conversationally.'[*]

It was his ebullience too which lay behind Engineer's rare mistakes. The most costly of these occurred when India played Australia at Madras in the last week of 1969, this the final Test of what had been an enthralling series. India, who needed to win to square the rubber at two-all, were 95 runs behind in the first innings. Australia commenced their second innings late on the third day. They quickly lost Keith Stackpole and Ian Chappell, both beaten by late inswingers from the eighteen-year-old debutant, Mohinder Amarnath. When Australia resumed batting after the rest day they were subjected to a magical spell of

---

[*] As quoted in Sharad Kotnis, 'Hail, King Farokh!', *Sportsweek's World of Cricket*, July-September, 1976.

off-spin bowling from Erapalli Prasanna. On a glorious winter day in Dehradun, I was picnicking along the banks of the Jamuna with my family, listening in to the radio as Prasanna went through the heart of the Australian batting. He bowled the left-handed Bill Lawry with one that turned right past him, had the dangerous Paul Sheahan stumped, and then disposed of Doug Walters and Brian Taber, both caught low down at short leg by Eknath Solkar. Within half an hour of the resumption of play, Australia were reeling at 24 for 6, only 119 runs to the good. At this juncture Prasanna beat Ian Redpath (the last recognized batsman) in the flight as he made to on drive. With the batsman yards down the wicket and apparently bowled, Engineer jumped high in excitement. The ball missed the stumps by inches, and carried on for four byes. Redpath went on to score 63, in the circumstances a match-winning innings. It was characteristically Farokh; he should of course have been, in textbook fashion, covering the ball with his gloves. But that was the man. When he came off—which, thankfully, was most of the time—he was very, very good; but when he did not, he was horrid.

Ebullience was also the middle name of the English batting genius, Denis Compton. Like the Middlesex cricketer, Engineer had a sunny temperament and a carefree attitude to the game. Like Compton, too, he modelled for Brylcreem. I do not know why the marketing men believe that well-slicked hair is in keeping with an ebullient personality, but there it is—another great adventurer on the field, Vinoo Mankad, also advertised for the product.

In fact I only saw Farokh Engineer's hairdo on the Brylcreem hoardings, for on the field he always wore a panama cap. In other respects his turnout was immaculate: neat, short pads that ended a little above the knees, cheery red gloves and, in the fashion of the day, a well-starched shirt with collar turned up. (This impression of neatness was somehow strengthened by his habit of bobbing the ball from hand to hand, throwing himself little catches as he walked down the wicket between overs.) All this was at the beginning of play, of course. By the time stumps were drawn, the pads, hat and shirt had all become a sharp shade of brown. But, as befitting a Brylcreem boy, not a hair was out of place.

III

It is time now to emerge out of the shadows of Mihir Bose. A cricketing theorem I regard as all my own runs as follows: all wicket-keepers make good batsmen, because none of them have turned the pages of the MCC coaching manual. When hours behind the stumps have concentrated the eye, sharpened the reflexes, and alerted one to all bowling variations, who then cares for a straight bat?

As proof of this theorem one has only to look at the unorthodox but highly effective batting styles of the international wicket-keepers of the Nineteen Seventies. Take Australia's Rodney Marsh, that crouching cross-batted left-hander, as doughty a cricketer as any from Down Under, who played so many valiant innings in the late middle order. Or take his counterpart from across the Tasman Sea, Ken Wadsworth, a free stroking right-hander whose abundant talents were never fully realized: claimed by cancer before he had turned thirty, he was buried with wicket-keeping gloves and a bat, his coffin carried by eleven former teammates. Or take the Jamaican Derryk Murray, whose Cambridge education did not inhibit him from clouting Denis Lillee back over his head in the opening over of a Test match. Towering above them all was their contemporary Alan Knott of England, who was without doubt the finest wicket-keeper-batsman in cricket history. Knott ranks high among the batsmen the Holy Trinity did not like bowling to. He revelled in hitting against the break, hoisting Bedi over mid-on or cutting Prasanna past slip.

This thesis, that stumpers succeed in front of the wicket because they scorn the straight bat, is of course splendidly confirmed by the career of Farokh Engineer. To the Indian team of the Seventies his contribution with the bat was almost as critical as his wicket-keeping. Although some of his finest innings were played in the middle order, he is best remembered as a dashing opening batsman in the tradition of S. Mushtaq Ali and Krishnamachari Srikkanth. Like those two maverick geniuses, Farokh cared little for the state of the wicket, the state of the match, the reputation of the bowler, and (especially) the rule-book. A ball outside the off stump might be pulled round to leg, or cut over point's head down to the boundary. Yet, and this was the despair of anyone who bowled to these men, a cross-bat heave might be followed by a perfectly classical straight drive.

When in 1967–8 Engineer toured Australia with the Nawab of Pataudi's side, he made a deep impression on the veteran cricketer and critic, Jack Fingleton. The first time Fingleton saw Farokh bat, in the Adelaide Test, the opener hit a blazing 89 in less than two hours. Reflecting on this innings, the Australian remarked that Engineer took more chances than any opener he could remember in forty years of playing and watching cricket, with the possible exception only of the daredevil Englishman of the Nineteen Thirties, Charles Barnett. (Fingleton wrote this as an opening batsman himself, the scorer of five Test centuries in rather more sedate fashion.) But when Engineer came off he was a 'pure, unalloyed delight to watch.' As batsman and wicket-keeper, he was quite clearly the 'number one' man of the Indian side.

The first time I saw Engineer bat, he charged down the wicket to the bowler—Bob Cottam, who was a lively fast-medium—and lost his middle stump in aiming for the medieval ruins outside the Firozshah Kotla. In the second innings of that Test (played against England, in December 1972) Farokh figured in a brave century partnership with Eknath Solkar that helped keep India in the game. This was a partnership marked, as one might expect from two Bombay men, by a series of breathtakingly close-run singles. Engineer himself showed a strong preference for the leg side: powerful on drives, wristy deflections, and a hook shot that was all his own. Where the batting manual recommends getting inside the line, with right foot taken across towards the off side, and hooking downwards to fine leg, Farokh just stood up straight and belted the short, lifting ball in front of square. If he missed, his nose would have had something to show for it, but he apparently never did.

Two years later, India played the West Indies in New Delhi, a match Engineer has especial reason to remember. The night before the Test, the host association threw a party for both teams, at which Ram Prakash Mehra, the grey eminence of cricket in the capital, and a powerful figure in the Board of Control for Cricket in India, announced that Engineer had been chosen to lead India for the Delhi match (both Pataudi and Sunil Gavaskar, captain and vice-captain respectively, had previously reported unfit). The wicket-keeper was overjoyed—this was to him just reward for thirteen years of devoted service to Indian cricket—and beaming broadly, he accepted congratulations all round.

No one knows to this day on what authority R. P. Mehra made his announcement. But after hectic consultations the decision was upturned overnight, and the next morning it was Venkatraghavan who went out to toss with Clive Lloyd. (Venkat was to be subject in turn to the whims of Indian cricket officials, when he was dropped for the next Test altogether.) Engineer manfully suppressed his disappointment, kept wickets without blemish through a long West Indian innings, and scored a dashing 75 in his own second knock.

Early on in that innings, Engineer was hit a fierce blow on

the head by a bouncer from Andy Roberts. So hard is Farokh's head, however, that the ball flew high off the skull to land yards inside the fine leg boundary (I have sometimes wondered whether the umpire would have signalled *six* leg-byes had the ball carried over the ropes). This was the over before lunch, and after running repairs, Farokh, to our surprise, strode briskly out to resume his innings. India were a massive 273 runs behind on the first innings, and the wicket-keeper now joined the debutant Parthasarathy Sharma in a brave, counter-attacking partnership. Then Sharma was run out one run short of what would have been his second half-century of the match, and Farokh was subject to a merciless but quite unfair round of booing. He had refused to run a suicidal single, after his partner had played the ball to Vivian Richards at cover point. It was clearly Sharma's fault, but the thirty rupee stand (where I sat) turned on Farokh, substituting 'Engineer Hai Hai' for their previous chant of 'Dilli Police Hai Hai'. Undeterred, he kept hooking the fast bowlers, disregarding the crowd and the knock on the head from Roberts, and also repeatedly cut Lance Gibbs from off the stumps. At length he tried the shot once too often, and was bowled. Engineer's courageous knock had recalled an innings played by another Indian wicket-keeper some forty years before: Dilawar Hussain, who in a Calcutta Test had returned to bat, swathed in bandages, and scored a half century after being hit on the head by a bouncer from the England fast bowler, Stan Nichols.

In both these Test matches at New Delhi, despite handsome half-centuries by Engineer, India lost. At the Oval in July 1971, Farokh scored a brave 59 in India's first innings, adding 97 runs in partnership with Solkar. India still conceded a first innings lead of 71, but were resoundingly brought back into the match by the right arm of B.S. Chandrasekhar. When India batted again Engineer played the most valuable innings of his career—a mere 28 not out, an apparently modest contribution without which his side might never have won. On a turning wicket, he arrived at the crease with his side placed at 124 for 4, still 49 runs away from their target. Illingworth and Underwood, two outstanding spin bowlers who knew the conditions intimately, pressed hard, but Farokh took his chances. He attacked with gusto at one end and, while Viswanath played soundly at the other, took India to victory. Ironically, Engineer had been only a last minute inclusion for the tour.

Farokh's most famous innings in India, however, had been played in Madras five years previously. He had been out of the Indian team for a while, when he was surprisingly recalled for the final Test of the series against a West Indies side led by Garfield Sobers. On the first morning, with his international career at stake, Engineer went to open the innings against an attack comprising Wesley Hall, Charlie Griffith, Garfield Sobers and Lance Gibbs—four reputations to daunt any batsman, but not Farokh. A most interested spectator was N. Ram, now an imperious editor, but then a Madras University wicket-keeper-batsman deputed by his magazine to cover his first Test. Within moments of play, wrote the young journalist, Engineer had 'punched a half volley from Griffith to the bowler's right, left him standing with a straight drive flashing past his left hand and slashed a rising ball from Sobers through the slips for four.' Playing the way he would in a Kanga League match, Farokh flayed four truly great bowlers to all parts of Chepauk. He was 94 not out at lunch; had he had a little more of the strike in the last twenty minutes before the interval, he would have joined one of the most select lists in cricket, of those who have hit a hundred before lunch on the first day of a Test match.

Engineer was a last minute selection for this Madras Test, chosen to replace that other swashbuckling wicket-keeper-batsman, Budhi Kunderan. He was, in a manner of speaking, paying back his rival in his own coin, for in a Test, also played at Madras but some three years before (the first of a series against

England), Farokh had reported ill on the eve of the match. In his novel, *The Shadow Lines,* Amitav Ghosh remembers how he received the news, as he was getting ready to go to school in distant Calcutta:

> 'The morning newspaper had said that Farokh Engineer was injured and would not be playing; in his place they had included someone called Budhi Kunderan. This was worrying news: Engineer was our hero, the swashbuckler of our side. I'd never heard of Kunderan: without Engineer I couldn't see that we had a ghost of a chance.'

Not a ghost of a chance. But after India had won the toss, the unknown Kunderan (unknown to Amitav Ghosh at any rate) proceeded to hit a dazzling 170 not out by the close, a profusion of shots flowing from an eccentric but well-seasoned blade. He finished with 192, and it was some time before Engineer sported an India cap again.

Kunderan was not quite as good behind the stumps as Farokh, but he batted in the characteristic spirit and style of all Indian wicket-keepers: to quote P.N. Sundaresan, with his bat 'more than a trifle aslant', his feet 'not often near the pitch of the ball'. In 1963, Shashi Tharoor, then a boy of seven, and another novelist-in-the-making, was taken to the Brabourne Stadium to watch India play England. This was the Test immediately following Kunderan's match in Madras. The home side won the toss, and within minutes Budhi had hooked the fast bowler Jim Price for a four and a six. After these mighty blows he repeated the shot a third time, only to send up a skier to mid-on. As Tharoor remembered it thirty years later, the batsman 'had begun running while the ball was in the air. When it was held, he continued running, threw his bat up skywards with a whoop of exuberance, caught it as it came down and ran into the pavilion. It was exhilarating stuff, and it made me a fan for life.'

IV

Farokh Engineer's immediate predecessor in the Bombay and Indian team was Naren (N.S.) Tamhane, a stumper very different in technique and character. Tamhane had been a student of King George's School in Dadar, a famous nursery of Bombay cricket, where (in the absence of Jesuits) he had learnt to keep wickets before he had finished with the alphabet. He left school to join Shivaji Park Gymkhana, and in time to form a remarkable partnership for club, state and country with the leg-break bowler, Subhas Gupte. Quiet, unobtrusive and superbly efficient, Tamhane is reckoned by some judges to be the greatest of all Indian wicket-keepers. One of the wisest of them all, Vijay Merchant, even said that Tamhane was as safe as the Bank of England.

The man Tamhane took over from was more akin in personality to the man he was to hand over to. This was D.D. Hindlekar, who toured England with the Indian team in 1936 and again a decade later. 'Darfu' Hindlekar was also at his best when standing up to the stumps, whether to the brisk medium pace of Lala Amarnath or the left-arm slows of Vinoo Mankad. S.K. Gurunathan remembered him as a character who wore his cap at a rakish angle and would engage the batsman in friendly conversation even 'if he was going to send him back off the next ball with a superb piece of stumping or a smart catch.'

Hindlekar was also a capable performer in front of the stumps, batting (in the manner of W.G. Grace) with his left toe cocked up in the air as the bowler ran up to bowl. In his first Test, against England at Lord's in 1936, he was asked to open with Vijay Merchant. Ten years later, he was down at number eleven, when he came in to save a Test at The Oval. With a quarter of an hour left for play, he and 'Ranga' Sohoni stood between England and victory. As John Arlott reported it, 'Hindlekar rolled out to the wicket, his eyes luminous with his blend of humour and artfulness to join S.W. Sohoni. The two

men played Alec Bedser and Dick Pollard with calm assurance.'
It was left to Hindlekar to see out the last over. He played the
first five balls defensively, but hit the last to cover's left hand.
Sohoni strolled through for the single, but to his surprise his
partner called him for a second run, muttering, 'One more for
my average!'

Old Bombay hands might contend that Farokh Engineer, at
least when behind the stumps, could not hold a candle to the likes
of Hindlekar and Tamhane, who were themselves the most
accomplished practitioners in their time of what is the most
arduous role in cricket. That is a judgement I cannot dispute or
confirm, but the fact is that Engineer was the first Indian
wicket-keeper to have achieved international renown: a name
recognized wherever cricket was played, and a member of Rest
of the World teams that played in England in 1970 and in
Australia the following year. This wider recognition was aided
by a number of factors. Hindlekar and Tamhane played little
cricket outside India, while Engineer, apart from numerous
overseas tours with the national side, also played several
successful seasons of English county cricket with Lancashire.
Again, India won Test matches rather more often in his time,
and cricket history, we know only too well, disproportionately
rewards winners. His association with the Holy Trinity also
reinforced his place in the lore of the game. And lest we forget,
there was also the man's ebullience behind and before the
stumps.

Engineer may have been the first Indian stumper to strut
confidently on the world's stage, but in the context of our own,
domestic history he might be better viewed as the last
representative, as a Bombay Parsi, of the pioneering stream of
Indian cricket.

A community numbering only in the tens of thousands, the
Parsis of western India have produced an astonishing array of
great musicians, writers, artists and scientists. They were also

the first 'native' community to take to cricket, and as early as 1888, a representative Parsi side toured England. Outstanding cricketers of the early days of Parsi cricket included M.E. Pavri, who as a bearded man of medicine and a gifted all-rounder was inevitably dubbed the 'W.G. of the Parsis', and Colonel Keki Mistry, a stylish left-handed stroke player Ranji once compared to the legendary Australian, Clem Hill. The organization of cricket in Bombay also owed much to the Zoroastrian community, and the game's guiding institution, the Cricket Club of India, was for years dominated by them.

By the Nineteen Thirties, the other communities had caught up with the Bombay Parsis. Yet when India played its first Test match in 1932, the pioneers were represented in the playing eleven by two all-rounders, P.E. Palia and S.M.H. Colah (two other Parsis were among the reserves). A dozen Parsis in all have played Test cricket, a remarkable figure considering the community's small size. This list includes two of India's best remembered batsmen, Polly Umrigar and Rusi Modi; one of its finest fielders, Rusi Surti; and one of its more successful captains, Nari Contractor.

There is, too, a line of distinguished Parsi wicket-keepers. They include Doctor H.D. Kanga, after whom the great Bombay inter-club tournament is named; and Bahadur Kapadia, the long-time captain of the Parsi team in the Bombay Quadrangular. Kanga and Kapadia were in their prime well before India entered the Test arena, although the latter did tour England with the side of 1932. Even so, Farokh Engineer was only the third Parsi to keep wickets for his country, following K.M. Meheromji and J.K. Irani.

Engineer himself grew up in the Dadar Parsi Colony, in the heart of the city. He had been acutely conscious of his community's contribution to Bombay cricket, a contribution that had been eclipsed in recent decades by the performance of native Maharashtrians. This is a transition encapsulated in the shift in

Bombay's cricketing headquarters, from the Cricket Club of India's Brabourne Stadium to the Wankhede Stadium. It is to me a fact of some symbolic significance that Farokh Engineer, the last Bombay Parsi to play for India, scored a splendid hundred in the last Test played at Brabourne (against Tony Lewis' England side in February 1973). But when he played in the first Test to be hosted at the Wankhede Stadium, against the West Indies two years later, Farokh, in what turned out to be his last international appearance, failed to score in either innings.

V

As cricketing appearances go, Syed Kirmani was a study in contrast to Farokh Engineer. He wore a broad-brimmed hat and outsize pads, while Engineer preferred a close-fitting cap and leg guards cut off at the knees. Opposing batsmen would recall too that Kirmani did not appeal with the same gusto, and rarely engaged them in conversation. Ebullience was not his middle name.

For all this, Kirmani adored Engineer, under whom he served a long apprenticeship in the Indian side. When Farokh finally retired, after that pair at the Wankhede Stadium, Kirmani very quickly showed himself capable of filling his predecessor's somewhat outsize shoes. In one significant respect he had been well prepared, for before he was capped for his country he had spent a decade playing for Karnataka alongside Erapalli Prasanna and Bhagwat Chandrasekhar.

One further advantage Kirmani had over Engineer was that his own Test career overlapped with that of Kapil Dev. While playing for Lancashire, of course, Engineer had to contend with high quality seam bowlers such as Brian Statham and Ken Higgs. But during his international career, and especially on Indian grounds, he rarely kept wickets to anyone whose pace was more than military medium. By contrast, where in the first half of Kirmani's career the Holy Trinity still led India's attack, in the second half they had made way for Kapil Dev and the left-arm swing bowler, Karsan Ghavri. At home and abroad Kirmani frequently exposed the spectator to the most thrilling sight in cricket—that of the wicket-keeper flying in the air to collect the swift edge off a seaming ball. This skill came spendidly into play during the 1983 World Cup, after which Kirmani was presented the award for the best wicket-keeper of the tournament by the great English stumper, Godfrey Evans.

VI

His familiarity with swing and seam notwithstanding, Kirmani will be remembered above all for his partnership with B.S. Chandrasekhar. The respected Australian writer, Ray Robinson, once called the wrist-spinner the 'wicket-keeper's best friend', providing him with dozens of stumpings and catches behind the wicket. Robinson had the orthodox leg-break bowler in mind, the artist whose flight and spin draws batsmen out of the crease only to leave them stranded as the ball, on landing, spins briskly past the outside edge.

Chandrasekhar was an altogether different proposition— much faster through the air than the classical leg-spinner, and with the googly as his stock delivery. Especially (but not only) on a turning wicket, Chandrasekhar was a stumper's nightmare; there can have been no other spinner who was as difficult to keep wickets to. Farokh Engineer, who coped capably enough in his time, liked to tell the story—partly in jest and also perhaps to cover himself—that the googly bowler was often unaware of what he was bowling. No one who watched Kirmani keep wickets to Chandra could believe this tale for an instant. He read the range of deliveries perfectly, moving with ease to the off side to collect the leg-break and outside the leg stump when he spotted a 'wrong-un' on the way. Chandrasekhar's bounce varied a great deal too, from boot-level to chest height, but it is difficult to recall Kirmani allowing the ball to jump out of or over the gloves.

There is a tale of an upcountry match in Australia, where a visiting Indian side played a team of youngsters from the bush. One batsman fractionally overbalanced in trying to drive a Chandrasekhar googly. Covering up down the leg side, Kirmani had the bails off before the batsman could turn around. He appealed for a stumping, but to his 'Howzat!' the square leg umpire merely answered, 'Wonderful!'

This story might be apocryphal, but a tribute with much the same meaning is available in cold print. It comes from the New Zealand wicket-keeper-batsman, Warren Lees. For the stumper, the most difficult period is the last half hour of play. This is the time when one is most likely to falter—after a day of intense concentration and exposure to the elements—but, notes Lees, "To see Kirmani keeping to Chandrasekhar throughout a very hot day and see him as sharp at the end as he was at the beginning was a revelation. *We found it hard enough to bat against [Chandrasekhar]. Goodness knows what he was like to keep wicket to.*'

I hold Syed Kirmani to be the best wicket-keeper to have played for India, with the possible exception only of N.S. Tamhane. Tamhane, of course, is honoured for his association with that other great wrist-spinner, Subhas Gupte. I once asked Abbas Ali Baig, who played with and against both, whom he would choose for an All Time Indian Eleven. Baig remarked that it would depend on whom one chose as the team's googly bowler in the first place. Thus one would opt either for the Bombay pair of Gupte and Tamhane or the Bangalore combination of Chandrasekhar and Kirmani—a choice, in other words, between orthodoxy and unorthodoxy all round. But, added Abbas wistfully, 'I would have loved to see Kirmani keep to Gupte, or Tamhane take Chandrasekhar.'

VII

Behind the stumps Kirmani was both safe and spectacular, very possibly the finest wicket-keeper to have appeared in Indian colours. Before the stumps he was, in confirmation of my own thesis on the subject, a highly talented performer. But I must not disavow a special interest in Kirmani, for we grew up, although ten years apart in age, on the same street; for me he was, quite literally, 'the cricketer next door'. In between his house and mine, in Bangalore's Jayamahal Extension, lay a small triangular park where he first put bat to ball. It was in this park too that he first learnt to keep wickets, using a brick in either hand as a surrogate for the gloves he could not afford. Soon he was spotted and taken up by that most devoted of cricket coaches, Keki Tarapore. But his technique in front of the stumps bore no marks of the smoothly run camps of the Karnataka Cricket Association.

Looking for all the world like a hockey goal-keeper, with his huge flapping pads, at the wicket Kirmani used the stick rather more often than a custodian of the posts. The bat came down in an extravagant scything motion, as he played a flashing drive past cover or swatted the short ball past midwicket. He had, too, a distinctive defensive technique: turning square-on to completely face the bowler, he played the ball down at his feet with an upright blade, in the manner of 'French cricket'.

Having grown up with Prasanna and Chandrasekhar, Kirmani knew all the tricks of their trade. He was a magnificent player of slow bowling, with an eye, sharpened by years of wicket-keeping, to match that of the quickest thinking of Indian batsmen, Krishnamachari Srikkanth. Like the Madras opener, he hit with relish against the break. The first time Bishen Bedi bowled to Kirmani (in a Ranji Trophy match between Delhi and Karnataka) he was carted to all parts of the on side. The sweep, often from outside the off stump, was interspersed with the lofted drive as Kirmani alternately sent deep square leg and mid-on in hot, but mostly vain pursuit. For a while Bedi carried on, convinced a mishit was imminent, but in the end had to take himself off in disgust.

I write of this innings, which I watched, from a distance of twenty years, but for a later Kirmani cameo against high-class slow bowling I took the precaution of taking notes. On a surface that resembled a wrestling pit, Kirmani was batting for Karnataka against Tamil Nadu in a Ranji Trophy match in 1988. The wicket was so bad that Tamil Nadu opened the attack with the slow left-armer, S. Vasudevan, a skilled and greatly experienced bowler. Kirmani came in to bat after Karnataka had lost a wicket in the first over. Two decades of first-class cricket had not dimmed his eye or altered his methods. Vasudevan was first square driven for four and then, in a characteristic Kirmani swat, pulled past mid-on. A slash past point and a lofted boundary (high and wide of mid-on) followed immediately, and then the Test off-spinner, Venkatramana, was swept fine for another four. Kirmani had six boundaries in his 30 (made out of 38) before a ball from Vasudevan hit a divot and came in sharply to take the off stump.

Through these unorthodox but uniquely effective methods Kirmani contrived a batting record in Test cricket almost as good as his predecessor's. His mastery of spin aside, he handled fast bowlers with more skill, and a great deal more courage, than several accredited opening batsmen. I have vivid memories of Kirmani square driving Jeff Thomson in Australia in the series of 1977–8, and in a pre-helmeted age, of defying Imran Khan for nearly three hours in a heroic effort to save a Test match at Lahore the next winter.

VII

Kirmani last played for India in 1985, but for several years afterwards his return to Test cricket seemed imminent. While he still hoped for a recall, I saw him one day during a Ranji Trophy match having a net while awaiting his turn to bat in the middle. Raj Singh, at the time the chairman of the national selection committee, passed the net, and Kirmani immediately dropped his bat and rushed to talk to him. It was an act in keeping with the balance of power between the two men, but I remember addressing Kirmani (under my breath, of course) thus: 'This man is only the present chairman of selectors, and will soon be forgotten, but you will be always remembered as the greatest wicket-keeper to have played for India.'

Behind the intensity of the remark lay a shared pin code, but there is in fact little doubt that my opinion is widely shared. The last time I visited Kirmani's home ground, the Chinnaswamy Stadium in Bangalore, it was to watch a limited overs international between England and India. Early on, that doughty competitor and then a most valued member of the Indian team, Kiran More, dropped a difficult leg-side catch from Mike Gatting. 'Kirmani would definitely have caught that,' muttered the man in the seat next to mine—which was true, if we were speaking of our hero in his prime—but then he went on, addressing the unfortunate More, 'bring him back even today and he will keep better than you.'

So long as there are men alive who saw Kirmani keep wickets you will hear comments like that—and not only in Bangalore.

CHAPTER EIGHT

The One Who Wasn't There

Watching Kapil Dev bowl on recent tours of
England, from his own position in the
broadcasting box, Farokh Engineer has
sighed, 'I wish he was there when we played.'
The Indian Test team of Engineer's day contained five fine
Bombay batsmen, a stylist of genius, four great slow men, and
an irrepressible wicket-keeper. What it did not have was a
fast-bowling all-rounder. When tail-enders held up the spinners
through a mixture of pad, edge and cross-bat heave, or when the
opposing openers got off to a runaway start, this was a lack that
was keenly felt.

The truth of Farokh's remark is not intended as a slur on
Syed Abid Ali and Eknath Solkar, the two men who shared the
new ball when Indian cricket came of age. Let us not forget that
Abid took six wickets in the first innings of his first Test (at
Adelaide in December 1967), a bag which included the
formidable opening pair of Bob Simpson and Bill Lawry. And
on the 1974 tour of England, Solkar gave the great Geoffrey
Boycott as much trouble as had that other left-arm swing bowler,
Gary Sobers. But it is no disrespect to say that Abid and Solkar,
both men of courage and fighters to the core, played for India
chiefly on account of their batting and fielding skills. (Notably,
both came to the new ball late in their career—Abid had started

off as a batsman-wicket-keeper, Solkar as a spin-bowling all-rounder.) At a pinch, we looked to them to score a defiant fifty after the top order had caved in, or to take a spectacular catch close in on the leg side; never to run through a batting side.

Ironically in view of Engineer's feelings on the subject, Kapil Dev first appeared in Test cricket in the very series, against Pakistan in late 1978, when the decline (largely on account of Anno Domini) of the Holy Trinity was made visible for all to see. That is justification enough for including him in a study focused primarily on the Seventies. And it has been Kapil, more than anybody else, who has since taken Indian cricket from early adulthood to mature middle age.

II

'This is the story of a phenomenon.' That is how Christopher Isherwood begins his biography of the saint Ramakrishna, and that is how we may begin our appreciation of Kapil Dev.

The first sign that a phenomenon had arrived on the Indian cricket scene came on the morning of the man's Test debut, in October 1978 against Pakistan in Faisalabad. Viewing the match on television in New Delhi, I had never seen him before; nor had the Pakistani openers, Majid Khan and Sadiq Mohammed. In his second over, Kapil bowled a bouncer that rose rapidly and nearly took the left-handed Sadiq's head with it. This was very likely the fastest delivery from an Indian bowler since independence, and Sadiq acted immediately. He had just returned from performing in the Packer Circus, where helmets had come in vogue. Here, however, he was wearing a green Pakistani cap, and Majid his usual floppy sun hat, as they prepared to face a day of slow bowling. But after that bumper Sadiq called for a helmet, which took a few overs to reach him in the middle. It is a wonder there was one on the ground at all.

As Sadiq Mohammed recognized, it was the *speed* of this

young colt that made him so exceptional in India's cricketing history. Some Indians before him could move the ball late in the air—though few with control to match—and perhaps Mohammed Nissar and Ramakant Desai bowled at a comparable speed, but without perceptible movement in the air. It was his pace allied to swing that distinguished Kapil from all other Indian new-ball bowlers. One might contrast him here with Mohinder Amarnath, a medium pace swing bowler who rarely posed problems at the international level. But at Kapil's pace, a lively fast medium in his pomp, batsmen had little time to change their stroke when the ball moved, in either direction, disconcertingly late in flight.

Kapil Dev's great glory was, of course, his outswinger. On a hot summer day at The Oval in 1979, Kapil completely beat Geoffrey Boycott's forward stroke with the first ball of a Test match—fourteen years later, the Yorkshire cricketer was still talking of a delivery which (as he put it with perfect sincerity) he had not been good enough to touch. His mastery of late away swing meant that Kapil tested the best openers on the most placid of wickets. In both the five day and one day game, the brilliant attacking pair of Gordon Greenidge and Desmond Haynes have always played him with care and considerable respect. Aware that a flashing cover drive might easily end up in the hands of second slip, and that the bowling at the other end, or after Kapil came off, was of highly variable quality, they have wanted above all to deny the Indian all-rounder their wicket.

Where the outswinger is his stock ball, in his salad days Kapil also possessed a sharp in-cutter which, bowled somewhat open-chested with a late change in action in the delivery stride, had unprepared batsmen doubled up as it struck them below the knees. (The in-cutter has gone out of his repertoire in recent years, when Kapil has instead preferred to bowl the inswinger, with no apparent change in body action, as his chief variation.) At his best he also bowled a fine bouncer, a probing delivery that even West Indian batsmen did not easily take liberties with. He has retained to the last his beautifully controlled sideways-on action, with such grace and economy of foot movement that Kapil must bowl fewer no-balls than almost any fast bowler in international cricket.

It is embarassing now to record that after watching Test cricket over twenty years, I have not seen Sunil Gavaskar score a hundred or Kapil Dev take five wickets in an innings. On two occasions, however, he came close to doing so. On the first morning of the Madras Test against Pakistan in which Gavaskar scored his match-winning 166, Kapil bowled a remarkable spell in which he accounted for four outstanding batsmen. The Test was barely half an hour old when Kapil had dismissed the Pakistani openers, Mudassar Nazar and Sadiq Mohammed, both caught brilliantly by Syed Kirmani, low to his left. Then Kapil changed ends, and with the sea breeze nicely helping his outswinger, subjected Zaheer Abbas to a torrid time. For two overs Zaheer played and missed before finally making contact, only to edge the ball to the wicket-keeper. Next, the prolific Javed Miandad was caught at slip off a beautiful away swinger. At this stage Kapil retired from the fray, leaving the pickings to his less gifted but equally hardworking fellow bowlers.

Seven years later, I watched Kapil in action against a more formidable batting line-up still. Following the 1987 World Cup, the West Indies came to New Delhi to start a four Test series. On a wicket that from a distance of one hundred yards did not appear unduly to help the fast bowlers, the home side were dismissed by lunch for a mere seventy-five. We had resigned ourselves to an innings defeat, but Kapil (still smarting from his removal from the Indian captaincy after the failure to retain the World Cup) had other ideas. In the third ball of his first over, the great Gordon Greenidge was caught plumb in front of the wicket, beaten by an inswinger. The dangerous Richie Richardson fell much the same way. In came the West Indian captain, Vivian Richards, with his characteristic swagger. This was a battle of giants, and the crowd held its breath. Kapil greeted the Antiguan champion with a bumper, and Richards, never one to duck a challenge, went for the hook. The ball flew high off a top edge to deep fine leg, where Chetan Sharma spilled the catch. Chastened by the miss, this young man (who adored Kapil, playing alongside him for the Haryana state side) took the ball at the other end, and ran through the middle order. The West Indies crumbled to 127 all out. Dilip Vengsarkar then scored a fine century, but with Richards in his best form the second time around, the visitors went on to win the Test by five wickets.

At the time of writing Kapil Dev has taken five wickets in an innings on twenty-three separate occasions, each time out of my sight. In an age where matches from Sydney to Sharjah are carried live into the drawing-room, I have sometimes been lucky enough to watch it happen on the television; at other times, to hear it on my faithful radio. The occasion I remember best was in a Test in Melbourne in the early Eighties. This was a match made notorious for Sunil Gavaskar's walk-out, after being adjudged leg-before-wicket to Denis Lillee. Gavaskar, who was then captaining India, pushed his reluctant partner, Chetan Chauhan, to the boundary edge, having decided to concede the match in protest. Fortunately the team manager sent Chauhan back, along with the incoming batsman, Dilip Vengsarkar. After all this India scored 324 in this, their second innings, leaving Australia a mere 143 to win, with a day and bit of play still remaining.

India took the field without Kapil Dev, who was nursing a strained calf muscle. An Australian win appeared a foregone conclusion, till Karsan Ghavri, bowling a lively fast-medium, left-arm over the wicket, had John Dyson given out caught behind (a decision that reflected as little credit on the umpire as had the verdict against Gavaskar) and bowled Greg Chappell first ball, around his legs. Soon, Graham Wood was stumped on the leg side trying to drive the slow left-armer Dilip Doshi, and at stumps Australia were 30 for 3.

When play began on the final day the odds still strongly favoured the home side. Their captain and finest batsman, Chappell, was out, but they had only a hundred odd runs to get, with batsmen of the quality of Kim Hughes, Doug Walters and Alan Border in reserve. But India could now call upon Kapil, who had recovered miraculously overnight (the three quick wickets might have had something to do with this). At one end, the attack was carried by Dilip Doshi, a most skilled and experienced slow bowler, utterly reliable in a situation such as this. At the other end, Kapil bowled a classically full length on a wearing wicket. He clean bowled four batsmen in taking 5 for 28 in sixteen overs (Doshi had 2 for 33 off twenty-two) as Australia collapsed to 83 all out.

III

I have not yet seen Kapil Dev take five wickets in an innings, but I did watch him hit his first Test hundred. It was January 1979 and India were playing the West Indies in New Delhi. I could not get a ticket for the first day, when Sunil Gavaskar (if only to spite me) and Dilip Vengsarkar both scored centuries. I was finally smuggled into the ground after lunch on the second day, moments before Kapil arrived at the crease.

At 353 for 4 this was a situation tailor-made for one who, to borrow a phrase from baseball, has always been a pinch-hitter. Almost immediately, Kapil hit the fast bowler Vanburn Holder over his head, a low skimming drive that thudded second bounce into the sightscreen. The off-spinner Larry Gomes was pulled to leg, and then cut delicately past slip. In a matter of overs, the fielding captain, Alvin Kallicharan, had set an ultra-defensive field. He was himself at deep cover, some twenty yards inside the boundary. Now Kapil hit a terrific drive on the up, theoretically a chance, that hit Kallicharan's outstretched but unwilling left hand on its way to the boundary. That was the only error in an innings otherwise free of blemish, as in two hours batting to the close Kapil had reached 94 not out.

I reached the Firozshah Kotla early the next morning, by now in possession of an elevated seat on top of the Willingdon Pavilion. Below me, the Indian captain, Sunil Gavaskar, was engaged in earnest conversation with Fatehsinghrao Gaekwad, a rare Board official with a cricketing brain to match his position of power. The discussion, presumably, hinged on the precise timing of the Indian declaration, which one expected to follow Kapil's hundred. That landmark took exactly two balls to achieve. Norbert Philip (a bowler yards faster than anyone Kapil had faced in India) was first driven crisply to the boundary at long off and next ball flicked with disdain over square leg for six. After his side declared, the all-rounder went on to take three wickets in a lively spell of swing bowling. India were however denied certain victory, possibly by an innings, by a thunderstorm.

Kapil's most recent Test century, his eighth in all, came in December 1992 at Port Elizabeth. Allan Donald—the Fastest White Bowler in the World—was given a fearful pounding, primarily at the hands of Kapil's distinctive 'Nataraja' shot: in between a hook and a pull, and played with the left leg raised and crossed in front of the right one, in imitation of Lord Siva's ecstatic dance on top of Mount Kailash. A more heroic hundred still was hit at Port of Spain in March 1983, against four of the world's fastest bowlers—Holding, Roberts, Marshall and Garner—to save India from what appeared to be, at the time he came to the wicket, certain defeat. Five years later, and also against the West Indies, Kapil hit a brilliant hundred off a mere 105 balls on the first day of a Test in Madras, a knock almost as important to India's innings victory as the sixteen wickets later claimed by the debutant leg spinner, Narendra Hirwani. Against a rather more limited attack, Kapil scored an extraordinary 175 after India found themselves at 17 for 5, playing Zimbabwe in the 1983 World Cup. Again, this was an innings without which India could not have won that match (or tournament). And it was played, in the absence of television cameras and live radio commentary, in front of thirty men and a dog at a country ground in the south of England.

I am reliably informed that a Chandigarh scribe is working on a biography of his city's most famous son, a book that shall doubtless contain lyrical descriptions of those hundreds scored at New Delhi, Port Elizabeth, Port of Spain, Madras and Tunbridge Wells. But the innings, or rather four balls, that most succinctly epitomizes Kapil's approach to batsmanship (and life in general) was played at Lord's in the summer of 1990. England, batting first, amassed a score of 653 for 4 declared. In India's reply, after Azharuddin had hit a brilliant century, Kapil crafted a strokeful fifty when he was joined by the last man, Hirwani. Twenty-four were still needed to save the follow-on; Hirwani somehow kept out the one ball he had to face that over. Facing the off-spinner Eddie Hemmings, Kapil blocked two balls, but then hit the third and fourth deliveries for six apiece. These two blows to the straight field had reduced the immediate target by half. Hemmings now hurriedly consulted with his captain, Graham Gooch. Three years previously, the veteran off-spinner had had Kapil caught at deep midwicket at a critical stage of the 1987 World Cup semi-final (a mishit all India believed had cost us the trophy); evidently Hemmings hoped he could buy the all-rounder's wicket on this occasion as well. Thus he flighted the next delivery, which, again, disappeared into the crowd behind long on. Hemmings and Gooch consulted once more, and decided that valour was the better part of discretion, which would have called for a leg stump yorker at medium pace. The last ball of the over was also tossed up, and astonishingly, Kapil hit his fourth successive straight six. The follow-on was saved, and Hirwani (possibly the worst batsman to play for India, always excepting B.S. Chandrasekhar) was immediately leg-before. It was not the all-rounder's fault that an abject batting display in the second innings cost India the match.

That was, without doubt, the most remarkable display of six-hitting in the history of Test cricket. Invoking an old Yorkshire bowler (with respect to W.G. Grace) Hemmings might have said, 'I puts them where I likes, and he puts them where *he* likes.'

IV

'Hit Out or Get Out' is a cry beloved of the Indian barracker, an imprecation hurled with relish at all incoming batsmen, C.K. Nayudu and Kapil Dev only excepted. Like the hero of Holkar, Kapil cuts a fine figure as he skips down the pavilion steps, lithe and graceful, swinging his bat in an exuberant circular motion. Both men are remembered for their legendary six-hitting prowess, yet their methods have been in the main quite orthodox: perfect footwork, and a straight, high back-lift in hitting the ball through the line. The drive, lofted or along the ground, might have been their chief scoring stroke, but Nayudu and Kapil could also play more wristy shots like the leg glide and the late cut.

Coming across a sheaf of tributes written in 1955 for C.K. Nayudu's sixtieth birthday, I was struck by the resemblance between his batting technique (as described by his admirers and contemporaries) and Kapil Dev's. This description, by an anonymous critic, brings out both the commanding nature of Nayudu's personality and the virtuosity of his strokeplay:

In many a pavilion and clubhouse in India there hangs a photograph of a cricketer, standing erect with bat raised, who glares defiantly from under the peak of his cap as though daring the bowler to do his worst. It depicts C.K.'s outlook on the game. [Nayudu] was a genius that brooked no opposition. There was no bowler to whom he would pay deference . . . . He would drive a half-volley and then next ball flick one off the middle stump to the fine-leg fence. When he cover-drove it was as though someone had wound him up with a key and suddenly released the spring. He would stand on his back foot, crash the ball past the bowler and then move across and back-cut the ball between first and second slip, a stroke that can be described as being almost posthumous.

I suspect that in at least some of those pavilions around India this photograph has been replaced by one of Kapil Dev. At any event, bowlers all round the world would have preferred to gaze at an action photograph of C.K. or Kapil than face them on the field, with a tiny, red spherical object as their sole attacking weapon. We have already been acquainted with the feelings of Eddie Hemmings, at Lord's cricket ground in July 1990; let us now append the testimony of an English bowler who came up against C.K. Nayudu at his best. Nayudu's most famous innings was the ferocious 153 he hit for the Hindus against A.E.R. Gilligan's visiting MCC side of 1926–7, an innings that included eleven sixes and thirteen fours. A victim of this onslaught was the great Warwickshire cricketer, R.E.S. (Bob) Wyatt. Thirty years later, Wyatt recalled Nayudu's ability to 'drive good length balls back over the bowler's head,' which made 'it very difficult for bowlers to keep him quiet.' But Nayudu was much more than a huge hitter of the cricket ball, for 'his perfect poise, high backlift and long, pendulum swing brought beauty to his strokes.' Wyatt could just as easily have been writing about Kapil Dev.

V

A swing bowler of prodigious ability, an attacking batsman of genius. But there is little the man cannot do on a cricket field. One day at Karachi, Kapil Dev topscored with 73 (made out of 98 while he was at the wicket) in the Indian first innings, and at once tested the Pakistan opening batsmen as they came out to play the last half hour. Then, fielding at deep fine leg, he ran a long way to his right in pursuit of a leg glance by Mohsin Khan, picked up the ball one handed, and sent a skimming return over the bails. 'What a cricketer!' burst out the commentator on Pakistan TV, a man not easily given to praising men from across the border.

In the evening of his career Kapil Dev is usually found fielding at slip, where the occasional lapse in concentration is compensated for by a lovely pair of hands. But in his youth he was by some distance the finest outfielder in the Indian team (I write, of course, of a time when the Nawab of Pataudi and Brijesh Patel had retired and Mohammed Azharuddin had not yet made his international debut). There was an extraordinary moment in the 1983 World Cup final, when Vivian Richards mistimed a hook shot off the persevering Madan Lal. The captain of India, stationed at orthodox midwicket, had to cover a good thirty yards, behind him, were he to reach the ball. It was a catch only the best of outfielders would have made. As Kapil ran towards the boundary the camera caught him with a broad grin on his face, a smile that bespoke of joy at the impending dismissal of the most feared batsman on the other side, but also of his own complete confidence in his abilities. It was a conceit this magnificent athlete could afford.

VI

In an essay written to celebrate the all-rounder reaching 5,000 runs in Test cricket, John Woodcock wrote in *The Times*: 'We should make the most of Kapil while we can. India have never had another cricketer like him, and quite conceivably they never will.'

We can have no problem with the first sentence of this statement, but there are some who might wish to enter a caveat with respect to the second. Think for instance of Dattatreya Gajanan Phadkar, the gifted Bombay all-rounder of the Forties and Fifties, handsome in name and handsome of countenance. Although he lacked Kapil's penetration and staying power, Phadkar could move the ball both ways at a lively medium pace—some older critics even claim that his control of swing is unmatched by the Haryana man. He will also be remembered as a brave Bombay batsman, with a finely organized defence and strokes all round the wicket, the scorer of Test hundreds against Keith Miller and Ray Lindwall at Adelaide and against Brian Statham and Fred Ridgway at Calcutta.

Let us go back even further in time. Nearly sixty years ago, Neville Cardus wrote thus of an Indian cricketer's prowess with the ball:

> [He was] one of the world's great bowlers . . . . He swung the ball now inwards, now outwards. His pace from the ground was vivid. He seldom pitched a loose length. A short run, a sudden rush of energy from a loose wheeling arm and the ball flashed down the wicket like a javelin.

This is how Cardus described an innings played by the same man in an Old Trafford Test:

> India were still losing when he came to the crease, and at once he began to cleave the English bowling with a bat apparently transformed into a scimitar. This was primitive cricket, yet glowing with a style of its own, a beauty which had its own mysterious axis and balance. [His] off side strokes were like shooting stars—all wrong in our English

astronomy, but all right and splendid in some other dazzling solar system. Most cricketers in the same situation would have gone into protective sheaths.

The respected critic E.H.D. Sewell, while echoing Cardus' judgement that this man was 'India's greatest ever bowler,' added that he was also,

> such a grand fielder. A real Constantine type, as supple as elastic, and as slick as a panther. He had usually too much bowling to do for the sides he played for to be always attuned to concert pitch at dashing about saving the analyses of others from annihilation. But even on one of his moody days a sheer joy to watch.

The man was, of course, L. Amar Singh. I lately came across the writings by Sewell and Cardus quoted here, but elsewhere I have assembled a sheaf of tributes to the Kapil Dev of his generation from his greatest playing contemporaries, men such as Learie Constantine of the West Indies (whose respect for the man grew while he played against him in the Lancashire League), England's Wally Hammond (who considered him among the most difficult bowlers he ever faced), and our own Vijay Merchant, who paid the ultimate tribute of naming his son after him. Amar Singh was without doubt the finest swing bowler of his time, a dangerous attacking batsman and, withal, a magnificent fielder. In all respects his cricket bears an uncanny resemblance to the preeminent Indian all-rounder of this generation. So indeed does his character. Lala Amarnath, a man most sparing in his praise, used to say of Amar Singh that '*woh tha dil ka* cricketer': a cricketer who played with his heart, but also a cricketer after Amarnath's heart. That is how Amarnath's son, Mohinder, might wish to remember his contemporary, Kapil Dev Nikhanj.

To my knowledge, the first man to compare the two was the

old Madras cricketer, M.J. Gopalan, once a swing bowler and bold attacking batsman himself. In January 1979, when Kapil Dev played at Chepauk for the first time, he did as much as anyone else to help India beat the West Indies in a low-scoring, close-fought encounter. After taking seven wickets in the match, he went in to bat with India perilously placed at 84 for 6, needing another 41 runs for victory. Kapil went about it the only way he could—hooking Sylvester Clarke and driving Vanburn Holder for boundaries. The most emphatic blow of all was a searing, lofted cover drive off Norbert Philip. As India won and Kapil walked off the ground, M.J. Gopalan exclaimed, 'He is another Amar Singh!'[*]

In February 1933, Gopalan had been one of the reserves when India played England at the first Test ever staged at Chepauk. After Mohammed Nissar dropped out on the morning of the match, through illness, Amar Singh had to carry the attack all on his own. On a perfect first-day wicket he bowled almost unchanged, claiming 7 for 86 in 44.4 overs. Long afterwards, S.K. Gurunathan recounted that magnificent performance wicket by wicket, singling out the ball that bowled L.F. Townsend, which 'swinging in late, went past his hip and just carried the leg bail.' Later in the match, when India were set an impossible 442 for victory, C.K. Nayudu promoted Amar Singh to number four. He hit a furious 44, which included a cross-batted six off the left-arm spinner, James Langridge, which went high out of the ground to drop into a tennis court outside—still one of the biggest hits seen at Chepauk.

With due respect to M.J. Gopalan though, the evidence suggests that in terms of class, Amar Singh was comparable to Kapil Dev as bowler and fieldsman alone. At the wicket he was explosive but erratic, an old-fashioned hitter, good for forty or

---

[*] As quoted in P.N. Sundaresan, "A Peer from the Past", *Frontline*, 25 February 1994.

fifty perhaps but not a man who could win a match off his own bat. As a more consistent, correct and versatile hitter, Kapil might be classed alongside C.K. Nayudu. But taken together, as batsman, bowler and fielder, Kapil Dev stands on his own: 'India have never had another cricketer like him, and quite conceivably they never will.'

VII

Amar Singh died, at the age of thirty, four decades before Kapil Dev began playing for India. Perhaps only a historian as backward looking as myself would dare couple the two. Kapil himself is quite accustomed to being compared with other all-rounders, albeit from overseas and of his own time.

Through the Nineteen Eighties, Test cricket was ennobled by four of the greatest all-round cricketers in the game's history: Imran Khan of Pakistan, Richard Hadlee of New Zealand, Ian Botham of England and Kapil Dev of India. All bowled sharp swing at above fast medium; all hit the cricket ball with rare power. Botham was arguably the finest batsman of the lot, Hadlee the most consistently successful bowler. However, over the course of their long careers both the Pakistani and English members of this quartet lost much of their bowling skill; they played for their country, towards the end, chiefly as batsmen. Richard Hadlee, for his part, did not always look an authentic Test batsman (he was especially vulnerable, as a firm footed hitter, to slow bowling), although he did play some blazing innings in the lower middle order. In this respect Kapil Dev best fulfilled the all-rounder's ideal, for he has always been good enough to play Test cricket in either capacity.

A detailed comparative assessment of these four giants could fill a good sized volume—this is not the place, and I do not have the nerve. But among his peers, it was perhaps Ian Botham who most resembled Kapil in his joyous attitude to the game. As cricketing personalities go, Imran Khan was aloof to the point of arrogance; Richard Hadlee, reticent to the point of sullenness. By contrast, Botham and Kapil are happy, generous characters (the Englishman's late remarks about Pakistani umpires and Australian crowds notwithstanding). Both enjoyed a huge popular following: Botham was once called the last hero of the British working class, and no cricketer, since G.R. Viswanath, is more beloved of the Indian crowd than Kapil. They were also, while they played against each other, great buddies. This is well illustrated in a photograph in Mike Brearley's book *The Art of Cricket*, taken during the 1980 Jubilee Test. Bob Taylor had been wrongly given out, and the Indian captain, Viswanath, after consulting with the umpire and withdrawing the original appeal, hurried to recall the departing batsman. That is the cameraman's focus, but in the background, Ian Botham (the non-striker) can be seen in amiable conversation with Kapil Dev, evidently about batting grips.

Another photograph of the two men adorns the cover of C.L.R. James' last book on cricket, published shortly before he died. Here Botham is pictured on the end of his follow through, having just bowled a bumper; Kapil, with swinging bat and body competely turned around to face fine leg, at the end of what has obviously been a very emphatic hook shot. This is a photograph that might only reflect the great Trinidadian writer's own, anti-colonial politics; I dare say there were other occasions on which the English all-rounder won cricketing encounters with his Indian rival.

VIII

Fifteen years after I had watched Kapil score his first Test hundred, I happened to be in the city of Bangalore. So too was Kapil, for India were playing Sri Lanka at the Chinnaswamy Stadium.

I had planned my trip so as to be able to watch the first two days of the Test before undertaking the work that paid for me to be in the Garden City, and then, with luck, to see the last two days too. Claiming my seat, forty-five minutes before start of play, I found in my neighbours (old Bangalore cricketers all) an unusual ambivalence towards Kapil. The fast bowler began the match five short of Richard Hadlee's world record of 431 Test wickets; eight hundred million Indians were urging Kapil towards the target, but my neighbours did so with more urgency than usual. They believed that it was the record which stood in the way of a regular Test place for their fellow townsman, Javagal Srinath—a place they thought would be all his own once Kapil had surpassed Hadlee's record.

Srinath is a prodigiously talented fast bowler who would be in my Indian eleven, every time; but his supporters' identification of the reason for his exclusion was unfair—for the man who had kept him out was the third spinner, Rajesh Chauhan, here included on a wicket predicted to turn square from the second morning. Anyway, India batted first, and assuredly made their way towards a target of five hundred. By the close they had reached 330 for 3, a brisk rate of progress. However, on the next morning they played painfully slow. Three greatly gifted strokemakers—Sachin Tendulkar, Mohammed Azharuddin and Sanjay Manjrekar—all batted as if a score of 500 was the sole goal, accumulating singles and playing hardly an attacking stroke against what was a tired, dispirited and mediocre attack.

Kapil came in to bat shortly before tea. He too started slowly, but after the interval began shedding his inhibitions. Perhaps to indicate his own contempt for that epic goal, he played a reverse sweep to get his team to five hundred. It was to my knowledge the first time he had played that shot in public, so to speak, but thenceforth the match came alive. The off-spinner, Muttiah Muralidharan, had been bowling all day, economically to a seven-two field. Tendulkar and Azhar had not found it possible to break free of his restrictive grip, but Kapil could. Muralidharan was glanced twice for four, delicately and very fine and then, with a spring in the batsman's step and that glorious, free flowing swing and follow through of the bat, hit straight for six. For those who know the ground, the ball actually struck the roof of the high BEML stand. It was a terrific blow; in twenty years of watching cricket at the Chinnaswamy Stadium, I had not seen a hit such as this. Another fierce straight drive followed; a low, skimming stroke that was theoretically a caught and bowled chance—Murali stuck out a hand and then quickly withdrew it, the ball striking the boundary boards, on the second bounce, with a resounding thud. Then Kapil turned his attention to the left-arm spinner, Don Anurasiri, whom he swept for four and six before cutting him past point for a third boundary. In a dazzling cameo Kapil had unfolded a range of shots. As soon as he reached fifty, Azharuddin declared.

An hour was left for play. In his second over Kapil produced a peach of an outswinger that took Samaraweera's outside edge and was caught by Tendulkar at second slip. This was wicket number 427, and the next day, while I was away (at last) on work, he claimed wickets 428 and 429, two lbw decisions, of which at least one was out.

On Sunday, the fourth day of play, Sri Lanka resumed with but three wickets remaining in their second innings, still some two hundred runs in arrears. The five thousand spectators had come, to the last woman, not to see India win, but in the hope that Kapil would reach or cross Hadlee's target. The most interested of them all was our hero's wife, Romi Kapil Dev, who had taken the early morning flight from Delhi. She sat a few chairs away from me, rubbing her eyes from lack of sleep, her face a picture of nervous expectation.

Kapil himself was more tense than I had ever seen him, most uncertain of stride and delivery for one who has otherwise such a marvellous, relaxed run-up and action. When the wrist-spinner, Anil Kumble, got the first wicket the crowd fell silent, but then the opposing fast bowler, the lanky Wickramasinghe, tried to hit Kapil over the top and was caught at deep mid-off. One wicket to end the match, and one wicket to draw level with Hadlee. A hurried team consultation resulted in Azharuddin instructing Kumble to bowl wide of the stumps, to give Kapil a clear field. The all-rounder strove hard, bowling an over of yorkers which the experienced Anurasiri kept out. Romi Kapil Dev led a group of anxious nail chewers—clearly no one would hold a catch off Kumble, but what if number eleven dragged a wide googly on to his stumps? In his next over Kapil began with two wide half volleys of his own, but then produced the perfect delivery for the tail-ender—bowled quicker and shorter, it jumped off the pitch to the batsman's chest, to catch the outside edge of a bat brought up in self-defence. The safest pair of hands in Bangalore, those of the Indian captain's, were waiting to hold the catch.

As I walked out of the Chinnaswamy Stadium the sentry asked for my ticket, but I clutched it hard and dodged my way past him. I have no physical record of the other Test matches I have watched over the years, but this one I had to keep: to be disinterred half a century later, as proof that when Kapil Dev claimed his four hundred-and-thirty-first wicket, *I was there*.

IX

With a man as supremely fit as Kapil Dev one hesitates to anticipate the end, but it seemed to me that the Bangalore Test was but one stop of what was, if not a great player's last road show, at least his last road show but one.

Ten months previously, I had watched Kapil in what may very well have been his last appearance in a Test in New Delhi, against Zimbabwe in March 1993. This match was also won by an innings. Kapil's contribution to the Indian victory was modest (one wicket and a dozen runs) but late in the match I saw him, fielding at cover, do a marvellous imitation of the man fielding at point, Navjyot Singh Sidhu. Like a tiger stalking his prey, Sidhu while fielding crouches on his toes as the bowler runs up to the wicket. Once the ball is bowled, he rushes in with exaggerated small steps, coming slowly to a halt. Kapil mimicked him perfectly, but Sidhu, intent on the proceedings, did not notice him. The thirty-rupee stand roared every time; it was at least three overs before Sidhu became wise to the act.

That is the cricketer, and that is the man. With John Woodcock, let us make the most of him while we can.[*]

---

[*] These words are now infructuous, for Kapil announced his retirement weeks after this book was first released. The present chapter might thus claim the melancholy honour of being the first tribute to the most remarkable career in the history of Indian cricket. It will assuredly not be the last.

CHAPTER NINE

Traditions to Live By

There are Englishmen alive who have never heard of Winston Churchill, and there have been some Indian cricketers who (extraordinary though it is to relate) refuse to acknowledge that spin bowling is one of our Great Traditions. One such was the late Maharaja of Patiala, Bhupinder Singh, himself a fine batsman and a great early patron of Indian cricket, a man who both employed cricketers on his staff and donated the Ranji Trophy. In 1933, in the middle of the only (and brief) period in our history when the tradition was not alive and spinning, he was asked by E.H.D. Sewell why India had no quality slow or googly bowlers. He replied at once, 'It is only because they hate being laughed at. They say slow bowling means sixers, and fast or fast-medium stuff is seldom hit for six. So they won't practise slow bowling.'

This was a prophecy the extent of whose falsity has not been matched even by Indian astrologers reading palms or Indian psephologists misreading elections. But to be fair to the Maharaja, the Test side of the time was dominated by the seam bowling pair of Mohammed Nissar and Amar Singh (with two other medium pacers, Jehangir Khan and P.E. Palia, in support) and in his journeys from Patiala to Simla, and back, he had doubtless seen Punjabi youths emulating one or the other.

Moreover, as a warrior-like Sikh he would himself have preferred the direct and masculine methods of the fast bowler to the feminine, or non-violent, techniques of the spinner.

Four years after the Maharaja of Patiala's remark, Vinoo Mankad made his international debut, and for decades afterwards the Indian attack was carried by the slow bowler. Yet the Maharaja's views never entirely disappeared and there has remained an undercurrent of opinion that holds that only fast bowlers win Test matches. The day after B.S. Chandrasekhar had routed England at The Oval, in 1971, the *Times of India* editorialized: 'But we still need to develop pace. It is a necessary weapon in any battle with the giants and over-reliance on spin can often spell disaster.'

This current has gathered force in recent years, in view of the dominance in contemporary cricket of the West Indies and the great successes of our own Kapil Dev. The cricket chauvinist has come increasingly to believe that fire can only be answered by fire: Indians must therefore take to pace bowling, if only to learn to beat the opponents at their own game.

It is this line of thought which lies behind the setting up of schools devoted exclusively to the recruitment and training of younger fast bowlers. First in place here was the Pace Foundation founded by the MRF Group in Madras, whose non-resident consultant is that most mean and skilful of modern fast bowlers, Denis Lillee. Shortly afterwards, the Mafatlals set up a parallel pace clinic in Bombay, drawing on the services of the long retired England speedster, Frank Tyson. Purely *swadeshi* or indigenous initiatives have since been established at Gwalior—with the strong support of the town's patriarch and past President of the Board of Control for Cricket in India, Madhavrao Scindia—and in Chandigarh, where the wards are taken in hand by Kapil Dev's own coach, Desh Prem Azad.

II

I remembered the Maharaja of Patiala when I switched on the radio at 5.30 a.m. on a cold December day two winters ago. India were playing Australia, halfway across the globe at Sydney, and to my disbelief I heard the announcement that we had gone into the match with four specialist seam bowlers, but no spinner. (India had already been beaten in the first two Tests of the series.) Now, in the absence of one Great Tradition, that of spin bowling, the other excelled itself: through a solid double hundred by Ravi Shastri and a dashing 148 (not out) by the eighteen-year-old Sachin Tendulkar—both Bombay batsmen—India found itself in a winning position, with Australia having to bat through the last day to save the match. But on a turning wicket, as Alan Border and company battled on, the only spinners available were the two Bombay batsmen. Although Ravi Shastri (who had, indeed, started life as a slow bowler) did well to claim four wickets, he lacked support from the other end. Then, in desperation, the Indian skipper threw the ball to his part-time off-spinner, Tendulkar. This, truly, was asking one tradition to do the work of two, a task beyond even this precociously gifted cricketer. The boy wonder spun out one dogged Australian (Merv Hughes), but the others held firm, and India drew a match they should most certainly have won.

It took a while, though, for the lesson to sink in. When India toured South Africa in the autumn of the next year, they continued to live by Bombay batsmen alone. Thus in the first Test at Durban a young, inexperienced cricketer made his debut at the insistence of the Indian team's manager, who overruled the captain and other senior members whose own preference was for a more seasoned player. He went on to score a matchsaving hundred. His name is Praveen Amre, and he had learnt all his cricket in Bombay. The manager who forced his inclusion on an unwilling captain was Ajit Wadekar, who, like the young man, was reared in the Bombay locality of Shivaji Park, and who once played for the State Bank of India team with Amre's coach, Ramakant Achrekar.

Wedekar and Amre are two Bombay batsmen who know precisely how, and when, cricketing traditions matter. As it happens, just prior to Amre's match, India had played a Test at Harare. This was Zimbabwe's debut Test, in which the hosts almost pulled off what would have been a most unlikely victory, being thwarted in the end only by a masterly defensive innings, spread out over nine hours, played by Sanjay Manjrekar. And in the Test which followed the tie at Durban, South Africa's bid for victory was thwarted by a composed century from the bat of yet another Bombay lad, Sachin Tendulkar. Three successive Test matches saved by Bombay bats: a sequence all too familiar in the history of Indian cricket.

III

In January 1993, the Indian team came to the Eden Gardens to begin a home series against England. At this point in time, they had behind them three conspicuously unsuccessful series overseas—in England (1990), Australia (1991) and South Africa (1992). The chauvinists and their pace foundations notwithstanding, three spinners of contrasting styles were now included in the Indian side, and a turning wicket prepared. This was done at the recommendation of the team manager, Ajit Wadekar, who as captain of India in the early Seventies knew better than anyone else how slow bowlers could win Test matches. With Anil Kumble (right-arm googly), Rajesh Chauhan (off-break) and Venkatpathy Raju (slow left-arm) taking seventeen out of the twenty English wickets to fall, the home team won resoundingly. As all India celebrated, I reckon the two most delighted men at the Eden Gardens itself were

Bishen Bedi, who as a commentator on television could express himself with characteristic gusto, and S. Venkatraghavan, who as one of the umpires for the Test had to keep his views very much to himself.

The next week, Kumble, Raju and Chauhan spun England to defeat at Chepauk and India had won its first Test series in seven years. The following week in Bombay, with the spinners again in the vanguard, England lost once more, for the second successive time by an innings. (In this match, the key wicket was that of Robin Smith in the England first innings. Smith was bowled by a Kumble ball which spun the wrong way—i.e. from leg to off. This for Raju Bharatan recalled a Chandra leg break spun past Peter Burge's bat in another Bombay Test won by India against Australia thirty years earlier.) Here was something for the Cricket Board to chew upon—the only spin academies in India functioned by courtesy of the Khadi and Village Industries Commission, and yet on the cricket field a trio of slow bowlers had led India to the most emphatic victories in its cricket history.

In New Delhi, I allowed myself a pat on the back. For in an essay published when the first pace academies were being established, I had warned that the new challenge to spin bowling would come to naught, and,

> our cricket chauvinists would do well to learn from history. In the early 1950s, Dattu Phadkar was sent to Alf Gover's School in London to hone his fast bowling skills: he returned a greatly improved batsman, while Vinoo Mankad and Subhas Gupte spun India to their first Test victories. Ten years later, after India had lost a Test series five-nil in the Caribbean, the Cricket Board invited four fearsome West Indian pacemen to play in the Ranji Trophy, hoping thereby to provide role models as well as help Indian batsmen overcome what was believed to be a national inability to play fast bowling. But in the next decade, it was the great spin

quartet of Bedi, Chandra, Prasanna and Venkat that carried Indian cricket to heights never achieved before or since.

The lesson was obvious: rather than look towards the graduates of the new foundations, the chauvinist might instead place his faith in 'Narendra Hirwani, Anil Kumble and the other young torchbearers of [this Great] Tradition of Indian Cricket.'[*]

IV

Mine was a prophecy rather less reckless than the one made by the Maharaja of Patiala in 1933. But traditions need each other, and to be fair Kumble and company can do little without the support of Bombay batsmen. The first great Indian slow bowler, Palwankar Baloo, rarely got more than a hundred runs to play with; the Holy Trinity were usually satisfied with twice that amount; but the spinners of today can often call upon totals in excess of five hundred. Such at least was the case in that home series against Graham Gooch's England side, when three Bombay batsmen batted brilliantly: Sachin Tendulkar, Pravin Amre, and the debutant, Vinod Kambli. The last named followed up a double hundred in the last Test against England with another in the one-off Test against Zimbabwe, played at New Delhi. The left-handed Kambli's scores in those two innings were 224 and 227. Each time he appeared certain to overhaul Sunil Gavaskar's 236 not out against the West Indies at Madras in 1983–4 (the highest Test score by an Indian batsman), but faltered when only a few runs away from the landmark. I was not alone in my belief that in failing to cross Gavaskar's score the young man was only paying homage to the greatest of Indian batsmen, and through him, to all masters of the Bombay School of Batsmanship.

In point of fact, Gavaskar has had a deep and direct

---

[*] See my essay, 'Cricket Chauvinism', in *Seminar* (New Delhi), July 1990.

influence on the Bombay batsmen of today. Thus Vinod Kambli had entered Test cricket as something of a cavalier, a prodigiously gifted strokemaker with one besetting weakness— the flash outside the off stump. In the Bombay Test of 1993 against England, Kambli was 20 not out at the end of the day's play. His teammates returned to the hotel, but the lad chose to spend a further hour on the ground, with Gavaskar. The master taught him to take his left foot back and across, to play the short lifting ball safely in front of the wicket rather than, as was his wont, recklessly behind point with feet well away from bat. By such methods Kambli scored a double hundred in the next day and a half, and one more in the next Test too.

The continuity of the Bombay tradition was also made most manifest when Sachin Tendulkar chose to play his first Test matches with a pair of leg guards specially made for shorter men, and gifted to him by Gavaskar. Watching Sachin bat, Sunil remarked, 'I gave him those pads thinking he would, like me, have to do a great deal of running between the wickets, but he only hits fours and sixes.'

This throwaway remark points to a distinctively new trend in the history of Bombay batsmanship. For Tendulkar, as well as Kambli, have at times displayed a ferocity in their batting that one does not quite associate with their city of origin. In the past, those Bombay batsmen who revelled in hitting against the break have had, will-nilly, to become exiles. Think, for example, of Khandu (K.M.) Rangnekar, that marvellous left-handed strokeplayer of the Nineteen Forties. Or of Sandeep (S.M.) Patil, a batsman whose technique and repertoire were all his own, but who played two of the finest attacking innings in Indian Test history: one against Denis Lillee and Len Pascoe at Adelaide in 1981, the other against Bob Willis and Ian Botham at Manchester the following year. Unable to withstand the stern and judgemental eye of the Bombay critic, Rangnekar fled his hometown for Indore, and the more welcoming embrace of C.K.

146

Nayudu's Holkar. Forty years later, when the Bombay Ranji Trophy found no place for him, Patil began a second, and triumphant, career with Holkar's successor side, Madhya Pradesh.

There is little fear that Tendulkar or Kambli will desert Bombay. It is not so much that the coaches on the Azad Maidan have become more tolerant, but that the game has changed and batting styles with them. Of course, both the Shardashram lads were trained by Ramakant Achrekar in the basics of batsmanship. Like their forerunners they have been correct in their technique, most discerning in their shotmaking and relentless in their search for runs, seeking always to convert fifties into hundreds and single hundreds into two. And yet, to see Tendulkar pull Philip De Freitas lustily across the line, or Kambli deposit John Traicos in the seventeenth tier of the grandstand, is to recognize an ability to destroy bowlers, and thrill crowds, that is unprecedented for a Bombay batsman. Made on a template of orthodoxy, these innovations in strokeplay are directly the consequence of the growing dominance of one day cricket. Through the Nineties, in Test cricket or in one day internationals, Tendulkar and Kambli will provide proof that cricketers from Bombay can save matches, and win them too.

The awesome strength of Bombay batting was displayed, as I was finishing this book, in a Ranji Trophy quarter-final being played at Bangalore. Karnataka batted first and posted a total of 406, helped along by a battling hundred from Syed Kirmani, in his twenty-seventh year of first-class cricket. In reply, Bombay were reduced at one stage to 174 for 6, apparently out of the match and out of the competition. Then, in a heroic rearguard action, the captain, Ravi Shastri, and the young all-rounder Sairaj Bahutule, put on 259 for the seventh wicket. Both scored hundreds, and Bombay won comfortably on first innings.

While Shastri's innings was watched by five hundred at the

Chinnaswamy Stadium, three of his colleagues, all batsmen, were performing in front of crowds in excess of thirty thousand, for India against Sri Lanka. Millions thought this just; for Ravi Shastri has been the least liked of Indian cricketers. I sometimes think I am the only man outside Bombay who wishes him back in the Test team. Actually there is another: the cricket writer and administrator Amrit Mathur, who reminds me that except only for Sunil Gavaskar, Shastri has the finest record overseas of all Indian opening batsmen, scoring Test hundreds in Pakistan and the West Indies and Test double hundreds in England and Australia.

Indeed, against the pace and swing of Wasim Akram and Waqar Younis, or Curtley Ambrose and Courtney Walsh, I would back Shastri against all other Bombay (and Indian) batsmen now playing. What he lacks in technique and range of strokes is richly compensated for by exemplary courage and a penetrating cricket brain. I recall watching him arrive at the wicket with his side facing defeat in a Test match played in October 1984 at Lahore. After Pakistan had scored 428 for 9 declared batting first, India were bundled out for a mere 156, with the left-arm fast bowler, Azeem Hafeez, claiming six wickets. Following on, we had lost four wickets for 164 when Shastri joined Mohinder Amarnath, with more than a day's play remaining and India still a hundred runs adrift. Shastri played out his first over with assurance, then walked down the wicket to have a word with his partner. Amarnath was recognized as the bravest batsman not born in Bombay, but the twenty-two-year-old Shastri was still making his way in international cricket, a spin bowler transforming himself into an all-rounder. But as the cameraman focused on the younger man I saw resolve written all over his face and I knew then that Mohinder had found someone to stay with him. The pair batted together for four hours, and the match was drawn.

Through the short and euphoric winters of 1992–3 and 1993–4, India trounced England, Zimbabwe and Sri Lanka without requiring the services of Shastri. This has led some to conclude that the man's Test career is over. But scores of 600 or more cannot hide the fatal flaw at the heart of the Indian batting—the absence of a Bombay man at its head. To score runs against Paul Jarvis at Calcutta is one thing; to fend off Curtly Ambrose in Jamaica quite another. At thirty-one Shastri is a young veteran, so to speak; still the Bombay batsman with the finest credentials to open the innings and save Test matches for India.*

V

With the consolidation of the Bombay School has come a revival of the other tradition of Indian batsmanship, that of the wristy stylist. This is a tradition at present embodied in the person and bat of Mohammed Azharuddin. When India began that 1993 home series against England, Azhar had been having a dreadful run with the bat. For the Calcutta Test he was retained as captain only at the urging of the new chairman of selectors, one Gundappa Viswanath. Azhar responded with a dazzling hundred, replete with rapier-like square cuts past point and those inimitable flicks on the rise through midwicket. The connection was apposite, for in more than one respect the Hyderabad man has taken over Vishy's mantle. Like Viswanath he is certainly more of an artist than a technician, finding the gaps in the field with the same ease and pinpoint accuracy. What is more, Azhar is not only a very fine batsman but also, like Duleep, Vishy and all other members of this 'little' tradition, a very fine human being.

---

* Alas, since this book was written Ravi Shastri has decided that the support of Amrit Mathur and the present writer was not quite enough, and exchanged his bat for a microphone.

Almost ten years ago I watched Azhar score his first Test hundred. This was on debut against England, at the Eden Gardens in Calcutta, a ground (and crowd) most beloved of all wristy stylists since S. Mushtaq Ali. Azhar came in to bat late in the afternoon, with thunder clouds gathering overhead. He hit one cracking off drive off Norman Cowans before rain drove the players off the field. When play resumed the next morning he and Ravi Shastri batted through the day, scoring centuries. We were thus privileged to see two batting traditions side by side (or stroke by stroke): the one careful and orthodox, playing through the line, the other wristy and innovative, making rich use of the wide spaces between midwicket and square leg on the on side and between point and cover on the off.

Azhar's most recent Test hundred was scored in Bangalore in January 1994, in the match in which Kapil Dev claimed his four hundred-and-thirty-first Test wicket. From my seat next to the players' enclosure, I saw a sight I shall never forget: three graceful stylists sitting in a row on a sofa, magnificent square cutters all. These were the Indian captain, the Indian chairman of selectors, and the match adjudicator from Barbados, the great Everton Weekes. When Azhar went in to bat, he was unnaturally circumspect, picking his way gingerly through the Sri Lankan bowling. One reason for this could have been the need to make sure that his side, batting first, scored at least 500. Another, the fact that he was playing in the Chinnaswamy Stadium, whose crowd holds that there will never be another like Vishy. Anyway, Azhar opened up as he neared his hundred, hitting some splendid forcing shots off the back foot. When he was out, he had placed his team decisively in command. Azhar walked back to the dressing room with the cheers of twenty thousand ringing in his ears; in the pavilion itself, the first man on his feet was G.R. Viswanath.

VI

When Azhar retires another stylist will take his place, one who likewise learnt his skills on bumpy roads and uneven patches of ground—the characteristic cricketing surfaces of urban India, which privilege innovation and discount the narrowly straight bat. Reared in more orthodox surroundings, Bombay batsmen will also continue to flourish, and sometime in the early years of the next century a West Indian fast bowler will concede the one hundred thousandth Test run to accrue to the city's capital account.

As for Kapil Dev, he stands above and beyond all traditions. This is the cricketer of a century—it is too much to expect another such too soon. What then of wicket-keeping and spin bowling, the little and great traditions of Indian cricket that are so inseparably intertwined? In 1986, Syed Kirmani gave way to Kiran More, a doughty competitor behind and before the stumps, a man who crouched low and came up appealing loud. After eight years as India's first stumper, More has himself been replaced by his Baroda teammate, Nayan Mongia—another little man with a big heart and a crooked but surprisingly effective bat.

But the future of good wicket-keeping depends crucially on the future of slow bowling. At first sight, there appears to have been a splendid revival of the first tradition of Indian cricket. As I have noted, the resounding victories over England in 1993 (and, it must be now added, over Sri Lanka in 1994) have been achieved by the classic, 'trinitarian' combination of a slow left-armer, an off-spinner, and a right-arm googly bowler. What's more, the role of Siva the Destroyer has been played by a tall, quickish and decidely singular wrist-spinner who comes from B.S. Chandrasekhar's own hometown of Bangalore.

But for all its recent successes, this Great Tradition is by no means as robust as it appears. In the opinion of the best judges, only Anil Kumble is comparable in class to the Holy Trinity. He has shown the ability to get wickets against all comers and on all grounds. But some of the others seem, in the words of an old Test cricketer of my acquaintance, 'to need a combination of a pitch the texture of a wrestling *akhara*, a total of six hundred behind them, and Kumble at the other end.'

Perhaps the game has changed too much and too fast for the tradition of spin to endure in anything like its classical form. Stacked against the slow bowlers of today are better bats, better wickets, the pressures of the pajama game, and the epigones of the Maharaja of Patiala. The first three trends cannot be fought, but we can at least resist the last. It is time to take sides. 'Tradition,' wrote Karl Marx, 'is a dead weight hanging on the brains of the living.' Now that statues of Lenin are being dismantled all over Eastern Europe, we can be so bold as to shut down our pace academies.

Index

READ MORE IN PENGUIN

In every corner of the world, on every subject under the sun, Penguin represents quality and variety – the very best in publishing today.

For complete information about books available from Penguin – including Puffins, Penguin Classics and Arkana – and how to order them, write to us at the appropriate address below. Please note that for copyright reasons the selection of books varies from country to country.

In India: Please write to *Penguin Books India Pvt Ltd, 706 Eros Apartments, 56 Nehru Place, New Delhi, 110019*

In the United Kingdom: Please write to *Dept. JC, Penguin Books Ltd, FREEPOST, West Drayton, Middlesex, UB7 0BR.*

If you have any difficulty in obtaining a title, please send your order with the correct money, plus ten per cent for postage and packaging, to *PO Box No. 11, West Drayton, Middlesex UB7 0BR*

In the United States: Please write to *Penguin USA Inc., 375 Hudson Street, New York, NY 10014*

In Canada: Please write to *Penguin Books Canada Ltd, 10 Alcorn Avenue, Suite 300, Toronto, Ontario M4V 3B2*

In Australia: Please write to *Penguin Books Australia Ltd, 487 Maroondah Highway, Ringwood, Victoria 3134*

In New Zealand: Please write to *Penguin Books (NZ) Ltd, 182–190 Wairau Road, Private Bag, Takapuna, Auckland 9*

In the Netherlands: Please write to *Penguin Books Netherlands B.V., Keizersgracht 231 NL–1016 DV Amsterdam*

In Germany : Please write to *Penguin Books Deutschland GmbH, Friedrichstrasse 10–12, W–6000 Frankfurt/Main 1*

In Spain: Please write to *Penguin Books S. A.,C. San Bernardo, 117–6* E–28015 Madrid

In Italy: Please write to *Penguin Italia s.r.l., Via Felice Casati 20, I–20124 Milano*

In France: Please write to *Penguin France S. A., 17 rue Lejeune, F–31000 Toulouse*

In Japan: Please write to *Penguin Books Japan, Ishikiribashi Building, 2-5-4, Suido, Tokyo 112*

In Greece: Please write to *Penguin Hellas Ltd, Dimocritou 3, GR–106 71 Athens*

In South Africa: Please write to *Longman Penguin Southern Africa (Pty) Ltd, Private Bag X08, Bertsham 2013*

CHASING THE MONSOON
Alexander Frater

An original, wonderfully entertaining and convincing account of an ambitious and unusual journey in pursuit of the monsoon, all the way up the Indian subcontinent.

'Alexander Frater's book is a wonderful amalgam of the beauty, strength, untamed power, frightening ferocity and the gentleness of the monsoon rains that nourish our lives and the life of our nation...'

— *Financial Express*

'It ranks with James Cameron's *Indian Summer,* as a potential classic of travel-writing on India.'

— *India Today*

'What is so good about Frater's writing is how believable he has made...India...Here's a writer India and Indian readers would welcome again and again.'

— *Indian Review of Books*

'Frater, the modern day Marco Polo, has managed to uncover the subcontinent's love-hate relationship with the monsoon. A travelogue as refreshing as a downpour after a long spell.'

— *Aside*

FROM HEAVEN LAKE
Travels through Sinkiang and Tibet
Vikram Seth

Hitch-hiking, walking, slogging through rivers and across leech-ridden hills, Vikram Seth travelled through Sinkiang and Tibet to Nepal: from Heaven Lake to the Himalayas. By breaking away from the reliable routes of organized travel, he transformed his journey into an unusual and intriguing exploration of one of the world's least-known areas.

'Because of the way he travelled, he was privileged to see things not on any tourist itinerary...*From Heaven Lake* is delightfully written and observed, a worthy successor to the accounts of the Victorian explorers and missionaries who tried to reach Lhasa nearly a century ago. I found it hard to put down.'

— Peter Hopkirk of *The Times* on BBC Radio

'Utterly convincing and, unlike other recent accounts of Tibet ... the most engaging and unexpected travel book of the year.'

— *Sunday Telegraph*

'The perfect travel book.'

— *New Statesman*

MALGUDI LANDSCAPES: THE BEST OF R.K. NARAYAN
Edited by S. Krishnan

The best of a lifetime's work — novels, short stories, essays, travel pieces and short non-fiction — of one of the world's finest writers comes together in one volume in *Malgudi Landscapes*. Skilfully edited and introduced by S. Krishnan, this selection brings Malgudi, the enchanting little south Indian town that R.K. Narayan created over half a century, to glorious and colourful life.

'The volume... highlights (R.K.) Narayan's talents as a novelist, a short story writer, an essayist, and a travelogue writer. An avid Narayan aficionado could hardly ask for more.'

— *The Times of India*

FALLING OFF THE MAP : SOME LONELY
PLACES OF THE WORLD
Pico Iyer

Pico Iyer is a traveller, and he particularly likes
places that the rest of us would make a point
of avoiding. This is a book about such places—
'lonely places', Iyer calls them, 'the places that
don't fit in', places that in their psychic or
geographic or political isolation become even
stranger and more remote as time goes on, more
possessed by claustrophobia and loony comedy.
Pico Iyer's world is unlike anybody else's. But
join him for a visit there and you are sure to
be charmed.

' . . . (*Falling Off The Map*) has pace and
style . . . interesting and very readable.'

—*Financial Express*